Strength for the Journey

Philippians 4:13 "I *Can*
do all things through Christ,
who gives me strength"

Heidi Benkert

Strength for the Journey

Journey

My Experience of God's Faithful Love through Cancer

Heidi
Benkert

With forward and contributions by Todd Benkert

Contents

Christmas 2012, 6 weeks before our journey with cancer began

Forward

For years, our family motto has been "In this family, we do hard." The saying is a reflection of our commitment to one another as a family and of the life choices we have made in ministry, foster care and adoption, and just choosing to live our lives in joyful sacrifice for others. The choices we have made as a family in our efforts to live for Christ mean that, sometimes, life is hard. We choose to work through and embrace the hard as the cost of following Christ.

Cancer was not a hard we chose. It came upon us suddenly and unexpectedly. Cancer brought a great deal of uncertainty and increased our need to depend on each other and on the Lord. We did not know what to expect over the following months and years, but we knew where we must find strength for the journey. Cancer is big, but God is bigger! I remember making the statement in church, "These are the times where we find out if we believe what we're selling."

In our entire journey, the Lord was with us for each step. He showed himself faithful. He showed Himself for who He is – He is good, He is powerful, He is able, He is for us.

As soon as we knew what we were facing, I set up a page for Heidi at CaringBridge.org.[1] While I made the first few posts, Heidi soon began journaling and sharing her experience with others. The posts not only chronicled her medical progress, but were filled with devotional thoughts of faith and hope and joy. Not far into our journey, people began to say to me that her journal should be published – "This should be made into a book!" I heard these words countless times. Heidi's words did not just inform others of how to pray, they were an ongoing testimony of the faithfulness of God. Each entry was a visible display of what it means to trust God in the midst of suffering. Heidi was ministering to others though her hope and faith – her waiting and trusting on the Lord.

When Heidi expressed her own desire for me to print out her journal so she could have a hard copy, I decided that the hard copy should be in the form of the book you now hold in your hand.

Except where an entry is labeled "Todd," all the writing is hers. I did the work of putting it into the form you see here. Heidi had expressed to me in the past that she didn't like when I edited her work because she felt the words were no longer hers. For that reason, I have kept the editing to a bare minimum. I have identified the bible translations used in keeping with copyright laws; unless otherwise marked, Scripture quotations are from NIV84. I have made minor edits to punctuation and spacing and fixed a typo here and there, but otherwise have left the writing in her own words, phrasing, abbreviations, and style. What you have here is 2 ½ years of Heidi's online journal – her experience of God's faithfulness in her own words.

A few of the entries from the journal are mine and are marked accordingly. In addition, I have included in two appendices an article I wrote for our church newsletter and a blog post I wrote about ministering to people with cancer. A third appendix shares a few resources we found on our journey.

I hope you will find this volume helpful. This is what faith looks like. I am married to an amazing woman – one who trusts Jesus and who shines the light of Christ each day. I pray that you know Jesus as she does and that you too will trust in Him.

Blessings,

Todd

1

Discovery – The Early Days of Heidi's Diagnosis

As we began our journey, here were our initial thoughts and the opening entry in Heidi's online journal. Todd set up the journal and the first entries are from Him:

We don't know all that is in store for us in the next few months. We do know that God is in control, that He loves us, and that He is good. We are trusting Him as we pray that He brings complete healing to Heidi. We will use the journal to update you on what is happening and how you can be in prayer for Heidi and for me and the kids and we may even share devotional thoughts as God ministers to us. Please join us in prayer.

February 18, 2013 (Todd)

Heidi went to the doctor last week for a growth on her collar bone. A biopsy confirmed that the growth is lymphoma. We will need a further biopsy and pet scan to get a specific diagnosis and treatment, but it looks like she will start chemo mid-March. Whatever the diagnosis, the prognosis for lymphoma of all kinds and degrees is good and much better than other forms of cancer. Right now we are waiting for answers, waiting on the Lord, praying for healing, and trusting Him. We appreciate your prayers for us. Blessings, Todd

February 18, 2013 (Todd)

Our next doctor's appointments will be on Thursday as we will meet with both the ENT doctor and the oncologist at University of Chicago Hospital. Please continue to pray for us as we are in the "waiting" period and do not yet know what we are facing until all the test results are in.

February 18, 2013 (Todd)

One of my favorite verses on prayer prompts me to request your prayers on our behalf. *2 Cor 1:10-11 "On him we have set our hope that he will deliver us again... You also must help us by prayer, so that many will give thanks on our behalf for the blessing granted us through the prayers of many."*

February 19, 2013

Don't really know what to say. We have had two friends use this site [Caring Bridge] and each time I logged in, I was looking into their lives. Now, it's mine. To see your picture on a site and know so many people love and are supporting you is an amazing thing. God is amazing and He will use all of this in ways I can't comprehend. He will be our strength when we have no more and He will teach us things through trials that we could never learn any other way.

Today, was a good day.

I think the kids are beginning to feel the effects of the stress that is to come. Please pray that God will bond them together through this time. Pray for Kaitlin, she started vomiting tonight and we really need to stay well, so we can go to Dr. appointments on Thursday. I know that God holds each day and so we press on one day at a time, following His lead. Thank you all who love and support us. Can't help but think of the current Chris Tomlin song - where it says – "I know who goes before me, I know who stands behind, the God of angel armies, is always by my side!" Thankful! Heidi

February 21, 2013

So this morning I reflect on life and where God has brought me. I think back to 18 years ago when life hit hard and I hit a wall. I remember thinking - Trust God? What does that really mean? I had been told it my whole life, and thought I knew and understood the words, but little did I know the journey God would be taking me on to refine me so that I would be ready for today's journey.

> I know that God holds each day and so we press on one day at a time, following His lead.

Practice makes perfect. We've all heard that saying. For most of us, someone was saying it to us, and making us practice. Well, I feel like that is what God does in our life, he allows opportunities for us to practice trusting Him! Not sure I'll ever get it perfect.

I spent days angry at God. Years struggling to understand how to Trust Him. God placed many opportunities in my life to teach me how to trust Him. Each time I took a step closer but failed in so many ways. My first instinct when life got hard was worry, fix it, "God make it go away!"—Fighting thoughts that tried to overcome me. Depression sought to rule in my life.

I remember about 8 years ago (after 10 years of practicing) the day came for another trial and this time was different from the rest, instead of fear, anxiety, anger, I trusted... I said, *"You have this God and I will trust you!"*

Today I read in my *Jesus Calling* book - "The more you choose to trust me the easier it becomes."[2] I believe this... No one wants to hear bad news, but when we trust God we know that He has allowed it, so instead of fear and anxiety we say... God, I trust you and we wait to see what amazing things He will do through the trial. Lest we forget Jesus said, "In this world you will have trouble, do not fear, I have overcome the world!" (John 16:33). If you are prone to think life should be easy, God never promised that, only that He would walk with us through the trial. So, through Him, we press on. Trusting Him means letting go, I learned that lesson last year, again :) It's so hard each time but it does get easier.

The funny thing is that we believe we can have some control – let me tell you, you don't. God is the author and controller of all things and I Trust Him! For God has not given us the spirit of fear, but of power and of love and of a sound mind. He will go before us and we will follow.

Looking back at life, there are many things I would not have chosen to go through, but had I not gone through them, I would not be who I am today. God will use all things for His glory. I'm just thankful that He loves us, cares for us, provides for us, teaches us and uses us. Heidi

February 22, 2013 (Todd)

CT scans tomorrow early (7am) and biopsy on Monday. Merrillville ENT doctor gave a general diagnosis based on probabilities – UofC ENT doctor wants a more thorough workup before diagnosis. Oncologist appointment was postponed pending results of tests.

Please pray for patience and freedom from anxiety as we await the results of these tests.

Isaiah 40:31 ESV *but they who wait for the Lord shall renew their strength; they shall mount up with wings like eagles; they shall run and not be weary; they shall walk and not faint.*

February 23, 2013

Funny how I wonder what types of things I'm allowed to say and write. How many of us think things but would never say them? Like today while in the middle of my scan the nurse asks - How are you doing? So I answered, "other than feeling like I might wet my pants and freezing to death, I'm great!" I mean really who gives you a blanket the thickness of a piece of paper and calls it a blanket? Guess they haven't seen the blankets at our house. I quickly realized I got two gowns because one was to wrap myself up in to try and stay warm.

Me? I'm not a real fan of hospitals, needles, gowns, and all the other fun things that come with being a patient, but I'm thankful for the care of doctors and nurses. God knows all our thoughts, every single one so I will work on sharing them with Him more and not so much any person around me who asks a dumb question. Sorry :) Loved the dye they put into your veins while your bladder is full and then you get this warm feeling, kinda like, Hmmmm... I wonder if I'm wetting my pants. all the while the machine is saying take a deep breath, hold it, breathe and relax. Have you ever been able to relax while having to pee and freezing to death?!?

See, no one said what a CT really was or how it worked, same with the biopsy. I keep thinking, no big deal and then when it's time, I'm thinking, endure, it will be over soon. Gotta keep a sense of humor, that's all there is to it!

So, the scans are over and Monday at 12 I will have my biopsy and there is a possibility after the surgery they will have more answers, so we will pray that upon leaving Monday, we have more definitive answers. Otherwise, we will wait another week.

Looking back at life, there are many things I would not have chosen to go through, but had I not gone through them, I would not be who I am today. God will use all things for His glory.

Our morning ended at a very unusual McDonald's. Like, what kind of McDonald's, do you have to go to the front and ask to be buzzed into the bathroom? Only the girls bathroom, not the boys. Really :) I was told, "You are at the ghetto McDonald's." Nice! and no refills on coffee, and lest you think about loitering longer than 30 minutes there was a sign for that too. LOL, the people were kind to us, probably thought we were lost :) It's all good! Glad to be home, tired but a quiet Saturday. Thank you all for your continued prayers. Heidi

February 24, 2013

Surgery in the morning in the new hospital at U of Chicago. I will be one of the first to have surgery there. Wish I were more excited. We did hear from the Dr. yesterday stating that my CT's showed only swollen lymph nodes in the collarbone area and chest, nowhere else. So, it is isolated and that is a praise. There is a possibility that after tomorrow's surgery the Dr. will have more clear answers for us, but if not, we will wait a week or so for the test results. Please pray for quick healing from the surgery as I plan to NOT give up my Ladies retreat and plan to travel on Thursday evening to Indy and enjoy friends, fellowship and whatever great things God has in store for us!

February 25, 2013 (Todd)

Well, we arrived to check-in at 10:00 for a 12:00 surgery... It's now 1:53 and they're "almost ready" to take her back to the OR :)

February 25, 2013 (Todd)

Well, with this being only the second day in this new (beautiful) hospital building, everything ran slow and took extra time as everyone learned where everything is and new protocols, etc. In any case, Heidi's surgery went well and she is now in recovery (I'll get to see her in a couple more hours).

We should know results in a week or so. Thanks for your continued prayers and encouragement.

February 26, 2013

So yesterday was not fun at all and today, so much pain. Please pray for pain relief and quick healing. Way more pain than expected and two incisions on my neck. You don't realize how much you use your neck muscles. So, hard to sleep, due to location of incisions and pain.

February 26, 2013

Thank you all for your prayers today. Tonight I am feeling much better after a stop at the ER for a few hours to take care of some extra issues that happened from surgery last night. No fun at all, but getting better by the hour. Thankful for much rest and pain meds and praying for more movement in my neck tomorrow. That would be great! Follow up with the Dr. next Tuesday morning and Lord willing she will have results by then. We love you all and are so thankful! Heidi

February 28, 2013

So, today I feel much better. Most of the pain in my neck is gone. My big joy for the morning is I was able to lift my arm over my head to put in a pony tail! The little things we do daily and never think about. Tonight I was supposed to go on my retreat and due to some other minor health issues and a Dr. appointment today, I can't go tonight. So, I'm resting and praying I will be well enough to maybe go tomorrow. So, please pray with me.

Please also pray for Todd and the kids, change and stress with in the household are hard. Pray for unity, peace, and patience for all of us.

I spoke with my nurse yesterday and Pathology has not given any preliminary results, we are hoping to know something by the end of the week, but if not my next appointment at U of C is Tuesday. Thank you all for your continued prayer!

March 1, 2013

Thank you for your prayers this week. Heidi is feeling much better and was able to go to her Women's Retreat this weekend. She's taking it easy, but the adverse effects of Monday's surgery are now behind her.

In the meantime, we got an early pathology report yesterday that affirmed the original cancer diagnosis. We meet with the oncologist for the first time on Monday and hope to have more answers then. Thanks again for your prayers – we appreciate them.

March 3, 2013

So, tonight as I climb into bed, I'm thankful! A long week for sure, full of lots of things I had not anticipated but it ended with a wonderful time of retreat! Refreshing time with God, a time to be silent, think, pray and worship Him. He is faithful and knows exactly what we need and when we need it. I'm thankful that Todd encouraged me to go and cared for the kids! I'm thankful for his support.

> Years ago, I came to realize that I cannot do life without Christ! I just am not able, I'm thankful for His constant presence in my life.

I've come to realize in the last week when in the hospital I kept keeping my eyes shut, at one point a Dr. asked me if the lights were to bright. I think, it's just soothing, comforting to lie silently with my eyes closed and not focus on the hospital, maybe it's my personal way of coping with the stress of pain. I really am not a real fan of pain, so we get through it. Life is moment by moment right now, enjoying the good ones and pressing through the bad ones.

Years ago, I came to realize that I cannot do life without Christ! I just am not able, I'm thankful for His constant presence in my life. I've also realized that I am a "one day at a time" person. As I bring to memory Matthew 6: 34 God says, Therefore, do not worry about tomorrow, for tomorrow will worry about its own things, sufficient for the day is its own trouble. God says - One day at a time! One moment at a time, I know and understand tomorrow has trouble, so for today I'm thankful and for tomorrow, I know God is already there and is surrounding our family with His love and care and many prayers.

Tonight, I will sleep well. I feel no stress for tomorrow. Now I'm confident when I walk into the Dr. office and he begins speaking reality will hit, then we will process and then we will move forward. I know God will care for me and my family, I know I will hate every moment of sickness or tiredness that comes with it, but I also know that for now, that is where God has me, this is the plan He has for me. I don't understand why completely, but I trust confidently knowing and believing He is going to accomplish things that He never could have accomplished in my life and those around me, had he not given me cancer! He will work all of this for His good and His glory, because I am His child and there is no better place to be than in His care.

So, what does tomorrow hold? trouble, of this I can be confident but God goes with us and we follow and we shall see what the end of the story is... blessings, because we are all so very blessed, there is always someone who has things worse, so I'm thankful! Night!

March 4, 2013 (Todd)

Well the verdict is in – after our visit to the oncologist we now know that Heidi has Hodgkin's Lymphoma – a serious but very treatable disease.

Heidi will need several more tests this week and then chemotherapy every two weeks for 4-6 months beginning in the next couple weeks. Our biggest concern is the adverse effects of the treatments on Heidi over the next several months and the impact that this reality will have on our children.

Please pray, yes for healing, but also...

- Pray that God would deliver us from anxiety over what is ahead
- Pray that Heidi will do well with the tests this week (one of which can be quite painful)
- Pray that Heidi would do well with the treatments and not suffer some of the more adverse possible side effects to which she is already prone
- Pray that I and the kids can step up and help mom with all that she needs
- Pray that we can model for our kids and others our hope in the all-sufficient grace of Christ
- Pray that we continue to handle each day as it comes with "our eyes up and knees down"
- Thank God for his blessing of friends, family, and church to support us during this time

We know that we are not the first to face cancer. I have been a pastor for a number of years and it's true that you never really understand what it's like until you go through it – and we're just at the beginning. Still, we know that God is good and that He is faithful. Even as we absorb the full impact of the news today of all Heidi and our family will be facing, we are trusting the Lord our God.

"I lift up mine eyes to the hills. From where does my help come? My help comes from the Lord!... the Lord will keep your going out and your coming in from this time forth and forevermore." (Psalm 121:1-2a, 8 ESV)

March 5, 2013

So, yesterday Todd gave everyone the technical update, now you will get life from my perspective, emotions, feelings, thoughts the whole thing. I figure me getting on here and writing must be part of the journey, part of my light shining for Christ, so here it goes...

Philippians 4:6 comes to me this morning, *"do not be anxious about anything, but in everything by prayer and supplication with thanksgiving let your requests be made known to God. And the peace of God, which surpasses all understanding, will guard your hearts and your minds in Christ Jesus."*

> I'm saying "I can't do this" and, yes, I'm countering that thought with the truth. I must, there is no choice. This is the path God has chosen for me and I will walk through it and come out on the other side.

So much to say about that verse alone, like how does one not be anxious? well by praying and thanking God amidst the pain and struggle. That is also how I find the peace that I feel I need each and every day right now. What kind of peace? the kind that will guard my heart and my mind. Oh, how hard it is to guard your heart and mind when the devil wants to take fear and let it over come.

I always would say that the biggest fear in my life would be loss of Todd, the kids, family. I am beginning to realize that physical pain is a huge part of my fears. In my mind I stopped that kind of pain after my last c- section, it just wasn't for me :) I have daily issues I deal with but after a while pain becomes a part of us and we learn to endure the daily issues.

This is a whole new ballgame. The unexpected is scary! Needing God to protect my heart and mind is top priority. I have had many struggles of the mind over the years, God has given victory and for that I'm thankful, but this is a new kind of struggle. Do you ever hear yourself, inside saying, "I just can't do that, I just can't"? Usually there is a choice involved! We often choose to not do it, because of fear or stress. But with cancer, there is no choice. I'm saying "I can't do this" and, yes, I'm countering that thought with the truth. I must, there is no choice. This is the path God has chosen for me and I will walk through it and come out on the other side. I'm not afraid of not being healed, I already have claimed that! The next 6 months will be life changing, and I've never realized what people really go through.

I am thankful for my Oncologist, he understood ME yesterday. He started talking about a bone marrow aspiration and core biopsy and he lost me, my mind was gone - fear, pain, I can't do this! I told him, he suggested taking a Vicodin before coming in for the procedure and after a bit of talking, he has now agreed Morphine and some other good stuff may be necessary. My body does not respond well to pain. Getting through this next procedure will be very hard for me, and then trusting God that the cancer is not in the bone. That would take me from Stage 2 to Stage 4. They don't believe it is, but we must know, before starting treatment.

So, I've decided the best help for me at this point is scripture. Please send your favorite scripture and know I will read and process each and everyone one, there is no way for me to face the path before me but with Christ leading the way!

Thank you all for your support, brings tears to my eyes as I read the guestbook today and some people I don't even know and they too are praying! Prayer is an amazing thing and I already know that I'm going to grow so much in understanding the power of prayer! Continue to pray for Todd, as he is such an amazing support and the kids as this too will be equally scary for them. Max responded - NO! you can't lose your hair! It's a reality. The Dr. said by round 2 of Chemo to expect it, so no more worrying about bad hair days and Mom's hair being all over everything and in the food:) We have to joke some to get through! Life will be challenging and hard for the next 6 months but God will accomplish more in the next 6 months that we can ever imagine.

"Though the lessons of trust I send to you come wrapped in difficulties, the benefits far outweigh the cost... The world has it backwards, teaching that peace is the result of having enough money, possessions, insurance and security systems. My peace is such an all-encompassing gift that it is independent of all circumstances! If you lose everything else, if you gain my Peace, you are rich indeed" – Jesus.[3] (taken from Jesus Calling) Heidi

March 6, 2013

So yesterday we got dumped on with a bunch of snow, Yuck! Although, I must admit it's very beautiful. It's March not December. Today I get to go out and "play" in it as I have errands to run and am just thankful to have a day I feel normal and have no appointments. Haven't heard from the nurse as far as the next appointments, I'm actually hoping they won't be 'til next week. I would just like to enjoy feeling good this week and weekend, and enjoying friends and family.

I want to thank you all for sharing your verses! What a blessing, hard to read through and not just cry! God is good and I'm just thankful! I think I will begin placing them on 3x5 cards around the house and in my bedroom, so God's Word is near when I need it most, every hour of every day! Thanks all, you are truly a blessing! - Heidi

March 6, 2013

So, the verdict is in. I got impatient waiting for my nurse to call because I really didn't want to have any more tests this week. Really, I just wanted to enjoy the rest of the week and weekend without the stress of travel and tests. So, my nurse was great and said she was thrilled I felt comfortable just calling her with all my questions.

So, here goes. Monday 8 a.m. I will go in for my port. This will be out patient with lots of happy juice. My nurse said she thinks it's best to do it ahead and let it heal, before Chemo starts. Sometimes she thinks they try to do too much, too fast. I agree.

Tuesday will be my lung test, and they are trying to schedule my heart test, and then at 12 they will pump me full of medication to get me through the dreaded 1 p.m. bone marrow. That will be a tough day!

Always much to be thankful for! Find joy in the little things this week, for you are truly blessed! God is good!

Then there will be one final test, the PET scan, they are waiting on Insurance to approve the scan, so we will have to go back for this, yet again. After all that, it looks like I will possibly start Chemo on March 21st and they will run on Thursdays, every 2 weeks, for 4-6 months.

So, after that phone call, my stomach immediately got a sick feeling again, but I will enjoy the rest of this week and the weekend and know that next week will be tough but God and His people are surrounding us, with love and prayers! Praying for that peace! Well, need to get off here, and get busy with evening stuff... Heidi

March 7, 2013

This morning I awakened with a sick feeling stomach. No matter how much you tend to tell yourself, you are okay, things will be okay, God's got this, your body still knows. So, I pray and process and move on with my day. Not sure now, that I really wanted to have things scheduled for next week, waiting feels a bit like torture. If you ever think you want to know the future, you don't! So, today I will review my scripture and get busy, distractions are good. I have read some blogs and I think knowing a bit more about the procedures is helpful, wasn't sure I really wanted to know more. Being informed takes away part of the fear of the unknown, even though everyone's experience is different.

I will know that Monday and Tuesday I am surrounded by prayer and that God is right by my side, protecting my heart and mind, I can't do this without Him, this I know! Thankful to have Todd by my side too, not sure how people get through things alone and without support, gives me a more clear picture as to why people make bad decisions without support, it makes a world of difference! Tomorrow I will go to work at the Women's Center[4] and if God allows me to feel well enough will continue to do this Ministry throughout my treatments. For, today... focus on today, it's going to be hard... Heidi

March 10, 2013

And the peace of God, which transcends all understanding, will keep my heart and mind! (Phil 4:7). I believe this and beginning to feel that peace in the last day or two. I do however find myself crying here and there, usually some moment I was not expecting to hit me the way it did. As I took Kate shopping, the laughing and looking in mirrors, her smile and the moments I have with her, so special. As I look in a mirror and realize that what I see today, I will not be seeing in 4-6 weeks, much will change, I will change, not just on the outside but all the way to the core. Life changes in a moment, enjoy each one!

Tomorrow we will head out early for me to go and get my Port. I'm thankful for the internet where I was able to see what that is and how it works, actually was afraid to look but seeing was helpful. I also read an article about a young girl and her experience with her bone marrow, they used the exact same drugs on her that they will on me, so that too have me a bit more peace that I will feel pressure but no pain. So, it's been processing one day at a time and I'm as ready as I can be. I will be remembering my verses and all the great promises that God is with me and praying too, that I remember nothing :)

My prayers are this - No pain during my procedures, quick recovery, no infection from the port and lots of time to rest the remainder of the week. Also, praying that the bone marrow comes back with a good report! I have other pains I deal with that yes, I would like answers for, but really don't want them to indicate cancer in the bone as well. So, peace as we await this result as well.

My nurse scheduled me for my PET scan and Echo or Wednesday and I had to call her immediately and say, no way! I think it's important to know limits and I'm thankful I know mine and we are not in a huge rush. So, my PET is scheduled for the following Tues and waiting to see if they can get my Echo scheduled the same day, pray that works out. The less traveling right now the better.

Pray for Todd to be able to balance all. He is my faithful driver, I don't do Chicago or traffic :) We are thankful he can take his work with him, but it's also a challenge to work and go, there are many distractions. So pray that he is able to get everything done these next few weeks and able to let go of the things he needs to let go.

As I hear others stories of their journeys with cancer, I'm thankful. Many spend weeks in the hospital and their Chemo is so much more intense. Even when life is so hard, there are always those who have it so much worse. Always much to be thankful for! Find joy in the little things this week, for you are truly blessed! God is good! Heidi

March 11, 2013

So, I woke this morning at 5:20 (felt like 4:20, with the time change. As I got out of bed I had to remind myself that I have cancer. It's a strange thing to keep telling yourself but it doesn't seem real. Off we went to Chicago, not nervous just ready for it to be over.

I'm realizing they ask you if you have questions and they answer them well, but there is always much they do not tell you. This procedure was not good for me at all. I keep thinking back over my day and realizing morning will be here soon and back to the hospital we go. Don't want to go! There is something in you that wants to just get up and walk away, not believing it's all true. Now, my pain at the moment tells me it's true! I feel like I have a hole in my chest. Take Tylenol, they say, I told the nurse I would be taking Vicodin. Don't think they get it, everyone is so different. I took a bit extra medication today during my procedure again. Very stressful, glad it's over.

Thanks for continued prayers, I'm ready for Thursday when I believe my pain from today will be almost gone, as for tomorrow's pain, I know I have much more insight from today's procedure and will be asking many more questions. I think there should be a way for Dr. and Nurses to have to go through each procedure themselves before getting their degree. Nothing compares to having been there yourself.

So, tough day again but thankful it will all be over soon! At least this part. Pray for continued healing and that I can mentally handle all this pain. Such a struggle. Heidi I will have Todd update next or else it won't be 'til Wed/Thurs. Anticipating much rest ahead.

March 12, 2013 - Update after a long day (Todd)

Well it was a long and exhausting day... and that's just for me. Thank you to all who have been praying for Heidi today. It was both harder and easier than expected. First the easier – the bone marrow biopsy that we were most concerned about, after a quite stressful lead up to the actual procedure, was not nearly as painful as anticipated and she received enough drugs to ease her discomfort, eliminate most of the pain of the actual extraction, and give her some needed rest afterward. I believe the relief from pain was a direct answer to specific prayer – Thank you, Lord! Also, I was allowed to be with her for the procedure and hold her hand throughout. (That's it in a nutshell – if you don't need the details, skip to the last paragraph)

The harder was just the emotional aspect of (1) having so much happen to your body in a short amount of time – simultaneously recovering from multiple surgical procedures, having a body that knows it is under duress, and having to deal with the anticipation of coming pain on top of all that you are already dealing with. And (2) having to convince doctors and nurses and others that although this is all very routine for them, it's a BIG deal to us – it's scary for us – and that she's in a lot of pain. Mostly, everyone is compassionate and understanding – it's just that half the time it seems like they don't GET it. Yes, our bodies are resilient, but all of this is quite stressful on the body, especially with a person with a history of not responding well to medications and high sensitivity to pain.

Heidi was stressed out for most of the day. The pulmonary test, again supposed to be "no big deal," caused no shortage of stress as she was asked to do some aggressive breathing exercises – forceful inhaling and exhaling – while having just had two surgeries in her upper chest. We had the nicer of the technicians as we heard another patient hearing instructions yelled to them in another room. She was patient and allowed Heidi to take her time and recover from a bit of panic. Got through that test ok.

Next, I called the nurse to see if I could get some anxiety meds – no go, but allowed her to take a Vicodin which did make her drowsy and took some of the edge off, but her heart rate remained elevated and she was scared.

We had a couple hours between procedures so went down to the cancer center and Heidi tried on and brought home a wig for when she loses her hair. The lady from the American Cancer Society was very nice and helpful. I think it will look very nice on her ("hot" was the word I used) when it is styled.

When we finally went upstairs for the biopsy, everything leading up to it was traumatic. We had to convince them to give her the drugs that were previously agreed on – convince them not to use the newly implanted port that was still tender and needed to heal – and convince them that the low dose of drugs they gave her were not enough. A lot of waiting in a silent room with the air conditioning blowing on us wondering when the whole thing would begin. The nurse and doctor were nice, but again, Heidi responds to pain meds differently than most people – always has – and you have to make sure people hear you! Don't suffer in silence! The doctor was very kind, but I think a little flustered by Heidi's panic and anxiety. He finally convinced her to let him start – and he listened! Not only did he give her the extra morphine needed – he used extra Lidocaine around the bone so that Heidi's pain really was at a minimum.

Afterward, we went and ate a late lunch and by the time I picked her up, she slept most of the way home. When we got home, it was my turn and I just woke up from a 3-hour nap.

A few take-aways from the day: (1) You must be an advocate for yourself – doctors and nurse do this every day and to them it's minor variations of the same thing – but YOU are unique and your experience is unique – if you need something, speak up until they listen. You CAN say "no" and there are legitimate times to do so. Spouses: If your husband/wife won't speak up – you do it for them. (2) Folks, I know some of you mean well and your intention is to ease the comfort, but PLEASE stop telling us that it's no big deal. It IS a Big deal! And just because Cancer treatment isn't as awful as it was 20 years ago, it's still difficult and stressful. And even if the prognosis is 95% cure, Cancer stinks! Don't minimize people's experience by telling them it's no big deal. I typed another whole paragraph to vent at the multitude of times I felt like people did not understand how hard it has been for Heidi, but I deleted it. Let me just summarize by saying that people need permission to not handle everything as perfectly as you want them to or think they should. And, I know I'm a pastor, but let me experience things sometimes just as a person without having to super-spiritualize everything. And finally, despite what I've just said :), (3) God is indeed a very present help in trouble. I spent much of the day praying silently for Heidi as she was experiencing trauma. I am thankful to be able to observe fist hand the tremendous faith of my wife. I am thankful for the Lord's presence. I am thankful that many others were praying. I know that he heard our prayer and answered by freeing her from what can be an extremely painful procedure. Please take a moment and thank God for answered prayer. Keep praying and keep encouraging. God is good. Thanks for walking with us.

> I know I'm a pastor, but let me experience things sometimes just as a person without having to super-spiritualize everything.

March 13, 2013

So, Todd wanted me to read his post today, there are just so many different feelings and emotions and you got a taste of his. Felt so bad, him having to see me and put up with me yesterday. Not a good patient, might be the label they would give me. I remember saying things like "if you don't give me the morphine and Ativan, I'm leaving!" :) Maybe I shouldn't have been so direct but I think I may have actually attempted leaving. She quickly responded, oh, no we will get you something. Then when the meds did nothing I basically wanted to know what plan 2 was. So, they did it again, same meds a second time. Just no fun!

Today, I awake and I'm so thankful it's behind me, I deal better with the pain of today rather than the unexpected of tomorrow. Thankful that my port pain is gone and now I've exchanged it for hip/back pain. I will stay in bed all day except to move occasionally. The pain is a bit unpredictable when walking so best to stay still. I'm assuming by this time tomorrow the pain will be gone, mostly. That would be great, I won't tell you how many days since I've had a shower. Please don't tell Ashley, she might not hug me :) They glue you together and cover you in tape and tell you not to get it wet or take it off for a few days, then do it again the next day. Yikes, ready for a nice hot, pain free shower. So ready! I see that in tomorrow's plans.

> I know this experience will allow Todd and I to minister to others in a way that we never have before.

So, the bed and I are friends today, and I thank y'all for listening and prayers. I know this experience will allow Todd and I to minister to others in a way that we never have before. I have never understood the fear of waiting for Dr. results or waiting hours in a room for procedures that "won't be that bad" The stress is overwhelming but knowing there are those praying, and knowing that I will never see most of the Drs. again, that I screamed, cried and yelled at :) very helpful.

Well, time to rest! Again, thank you all for praying us through yesterday. I don't anticipate anything being worse than what we have already been through. Thank you for meals and for caring for my children! Everyone has been amazing. Thank you for cards, and letters.

We will get through, I never doubt that, it's just the one day at a time thing. And the wig thing, not sure I'm ready for a darker color, we shall see, lots of adventure ahead, I'll call it adventure instead of... Yikes, not really ready for that either. Back to one day at a time!

March 14, 2013

Psalm 27 (KJV) *The Lord is my light and my salvation, Whom shall I fear? The Lord is the strength of my life of whom shall I be afraid?... For in the time of trouble He shall hide me in His pavilion; in the secret place of His tabernacle, He shall hide me, He shall set me high upon a rock... I would have lost heart, unless I had believed... Wait on the Lord, Be of good courage, and He shall strengthen your heart; Wait, I say, on the Lord.*

Today started with a shower! Praise God, how refreshing. It was not real long because I find myself very weak today from the events of the week. My pain is about 50% better today, I'm able to move a bit better but some movements are still a bit unpredictable and painful. My chest feels like it's been beaten a bit and the wonderful collage of colors appearing from the port and interesting. I find interesting what Drs describe as a routine procedure, maybe to them but the looks of this port in my chest is far from routine to me and my life. I don't mind the scars, I know in time I will heal and the scars will remind me what I came through...

> Pray for our children . . . Life is scary for them when the normal changes, we all deal with change in our own ways. Pray protection over their hearts and minds.

My heart breaks when I think of those whose life is filled with cancer... whose diagnosis is long term and much more intense. For the children who suffer and the parents who have to watch and are able to do nothing. Life is all perspective, we live each day not knowing what others deal with, so inwardly focused... well, I'm not feeling too well, need to sign off and rest. Trying to move a bit more today and eat more, need the strength and I'm hopeful tomorrow will be even better. Thankful for healing, although slow, thankful for a husband, I could not do this alone! Thankful for all your kind words, Caring Bridges does not allow me to respond to you individually or I would try. I am resting but if you want to call and say hi, don't hesitate, I'm only sleeping a small portion of my day, it's more about being still and healing. Back to bed. Heidi

March 15, 2013

So, Friday has come, it's been another long week. I am thankful to have less pain today and I'm even thinking about running to the bank. We will see how driving goes. It's hard to adjust to the fact that it hurts to move many ways and then all of a sudden it doesn't hurt as much.

Life is full of so much busyness. Please continue to pray for more healing over the weekend in preparation for next weeks, final test and first Chemo.

Pray for our children, they will continue to be affected in many ways in the days to come. Pray that they will have hearts that want to help and a spirit of unity midst much change. With 3 teens they have their own issues and struggles and life is challenging. Kaitlin being 7, she is just sad to see mommy hurting, but she is my big helper and we get lots of time together. Life is scary for them when the normal changes, we all deal with change in our own ways. Pray protection over their hearts and minds.

Pray for Todd. He has so much on his plate. Being full time Mom this week, with carpooling and keeping up with normal everyday stuff has been exhausting. There is so much to process in caring for a family when the Mom is unable to do the normal everyday things. We are thankful for support and continued prayers. Pray for strength and quiet times, midst the chaos.

I will speak for myself in saying you really don't know what it's like, unless you have been there. I've never been here and I'm seeing just how blind I've been to the deep struggles of those who deal with such devastating loss of some sort in their lives. Loss of dreams, loss of time, loss of everyday things we are used to doing. The list is long but reality is hitting home. I'm thankful that I don't fear losing my faith, I know it's strong and I know all God's promises and I'm thankful for all the reminders, but we are human and we still have human thoughts, fears, feelings of wanting to quit and just run and hide. If you have been there you get this.

We will be forever changed by what God is walking us through and perspective of what is really important in life will be changed forever as well. Praying God forever changes us, our children and those whose lives ours touch. - Have a blessed day, and please pray for Spring to come, I need it! Heidi

March 18, 2013

While reading a dear friend's e-mail this week, I am reminded that God allows us to experience things we would not choose for ourselves. He - takes us out of our comfort zones :) - He allows tough times. Thinking about this brings a passage straight to mind. Paul says...

2 Corinthians 1:8-11 *"We were under great pressure, far beyond our ability to endure, so that we despaired even of life. Indeed, in our hearts we felt the sentence of death. BUT this happened that we might not rely on ourselves but on God, who raises the dead. He has delivered us from such a deadly peril, and he will deliver us. On HIM we have set our HOPE that HE will continue to deliver us, as you help us by your prayers. Then many will give thanks on our behalf for the gracious favor granted us in answer to the prayers of many.*

I like the part about praying in this passage. I think for the first time I've really noticed it!... as you help us by your prayers... Then many will give thanks!

I have visited this passage many times in my Bible. Always reminded that the reason WHY? is so we will no longer rely on ourselves, we will understand that GOD is GOD (he raises the dead, he delivers us) and He will do what He wants to change us, mold us and make us into who He knows we can and will be. I like the part about praying in this passage. I think for the first time I've really noticed it!... as you help us by your prayers... Then many will give thanks! Such good stuff... it's all about trusting that God knows best... hard to do, it's a process. Thank you all for coming along side us, it's an amazing things.

> It's all about trusting that God knows best... hard to do, it's a process.

As for this week, I hope to hear from my nurse today for more details but some prayer requests... -We will be traveling Tues and Thurs to Chicago so pray for safety. I would like prayers for my port to feel really healed tomorrow when it comes time to access it for the first time. I want that to go well, since it will be accessed again on Thursday for chemo. -Pray that I will be able to sleep comfortably. Woke up frustrated this morning from my bone marrow. That area gets unhappy when laid on, not many comfy positions with my port and hip, with a bump on it. I convince myself that the pain I feel means - it's continuing to heal, and I know it won't last too much longer. Thankful for that. - Pray for Todd this week, He has his normal work load, plus two days in Chicago with me and then a team of people from Builders for Christ will be here all weekend as we are doing a Ground Breaking Ceremony on Palm Sunday for our new Church building! It will be a very long and exhausting week but full of many great and exciting things. In light of our crazy week and weekend, pray I tolerate Chemo well this week, that I won't get sick or feel any of the side effects. Pray for continued physical strength, and absence of anxiety.

I would like to be a part of the upcoming weekend, at some level. With Builders for Christ coming and our oldest daughter, Ashley, performing in Cinderella at the high school and (although I saw it this weekend, not willing to gamble how I will feel next weekend) I would like to be able to go with my family to see it again and feel well enough to visit. A blessed day to everyone, rainy and yucky here but thankful to be able to go out today and do a few things! Heidi

March 18, 2013

So, I will quickly update one more time today. From talking to my nurse, she can't say what my test results were from the bone marrow, but she said, she didn't think I had anything to worry about. (If you know what I mean) I think that is a praise then, but we will officially talk to the Dr. on Thursday.

I was very excited when she told me she was unsure (because that's not the field she works in) if they could actually use my port for the PET. I told her great, I don't want them to use it. She said either way, I could tell them I only want my port used for Chemo alone, no blood draws etc. So, I like hearing that, maybe I will get used to using the port and change my mind in time (they draw blood every two weeks).

So basically, I think tomorrow will be pain free, I can take an IV – piece of cake! So expecting to feel good, both Tues and Wed, Whoohooo!!!!

My nurse did ask how I did with the bone marrow and I told her I got a double dose of meds and she asked how long before they were able to get me off the table :) I told her I was fine. Todd laughed, he said it was just a bit delayed reaction, I guess I was pretty doped up, according to him :) afterward, yeah, whatever :) It's all history now! The less I remember the better! Well, I think that's all, Chemo Thursday will be long, they said, first one, lots of instructions, meds and stuff but soon that too will be behind us and we will have a more clear idea of how life will be for the next several months. - Heidi

March 20, 2013

So, even when we are in the middle of trial - God helps us, if we choose to see others and their trials, struggles and He empowers us to encourage them and pray for them. Today, I received 2 e-mails of families I love whose husbands have lost their jobs this week, another recently laid off. I sit back and wonder, what is God doing? I don't necessarily question why, because if we are His children, it will all end good, He promises! We just all hate the struggle, we are human.

> Know that God is in the business of Astounding us!!! That's what He wants! He loves you and if you let Him, He will astound.

Habakkuk 1:5 came to mind in the car today, I remember hearing Nancy Leigh Demoss, explain this scripture. I will say, that I'm no deep Bible scholar and I know that the circumstances in Habakkuk are different. All our struggles are different at some level, because we are. Sometimes we are in the struggle and sometimes we are watching those we love, either way - it's hard and I'm thankful for Christ.

So, the Lord says - *Look among the nations and watch - Be utterly astounded! For I will work a work in your days which you would not believe, though it were told you!*

I want to be astounded by God and His working... I don't think I always want to see what is to come... goes back to one day at time. God himself says, you wouldn't believe it, even if I told you :) He knows us so well. So, those are my thoughts! Know that God is in the business of Astounding us!!! That's what He wants! He loves you and if you let Him, He will astound. Midst trial and struggle, I'm somehow able to look at the circumstances and say, "Thank you Lord for answering prayers!" What? Yeah, midst the struggles, He is definitely answering prayers, Okay, not the way I would do it, but then again, I'm not God! and we can all thank God for that... and my update...

Yesterday was pain free (getting an IV doesn't count as pain anymore :) I was sore and tired because I had to sit for hours... No one mentioned when they put the glucose in, that you have to sit still for a short period of 90 minutes, What? I said... resting, thankfully there was at least a TV but sitting for long periods still is not very comfortable. So I watched a little of about 10 different shows in that time, we don't have cable, so I was exploring :)

I find myself in each situation becoming more thankful. As I had my Echo, I was thankful for the not so personal kind of cancer I do have. I laid there thanking God. If you've been in the hospital or had tests done, you understand that in the medical profession, gee... they see it every day, but in my world... well, it's a private world. I'm thankful for the few uncomfortable moments that will pass and not become the norm... My thrill for today is after 6 weeks, I was able to actually put a Hoodie on!!!!!!! It's cold outside and inside :) and I need a hoodie to survive, and it felt so wonderful to be able to wear one, I know small, but reality is we go through every day not realizing the comforts we have. Me too... I'm included in that.

I'm currently eating deep dish pizza, Todd and I got to go to Connie's for dinner last night, instead of sitting in traffic for hours and after another day of hours of fasting for tests, I was so starved!!! Decided, I wanted Pizza, since who knows how long it might be before I desire to eat it again. (big thank you to those who love and care for our children, you are the best and we could not do this without you)

So, when asked lately how are you? my response is - Today, I'm good! I am, as for tomorrow, Chemo will start at 1:30, my port is very healed and I have this great cream I asked for that people swear by, I've even watched a demo on how to put it on right so you basically feel nothing... I will let you know if it really works, hope so! I am not worried about tomorrow, others are concerned for me, but you know me. I will be concerned after the fact, if I don't feel well, yet to be determined. Today I will enjoy this evening with my family, do a bit of shopping with the kids and be so thankful for all the amazing people God has placed in our lives! If I forget any details (LOL, I probably give more than you really want to know) just let me know, happy to answer any questions. Heidi

March 20, 2013 – Todd's thoughts on the night before Chemo

Well, the emotion of it all has finally caught up with me. There I was, in the Christian bookstore. I read a few greeting cards from the "encouragement" and "get well" sections and I started crying. Reading those messages of encouragement and hope, based on the promises of God, I was overcome with a rush of emotion. It was one of those bitter-sweet moments where my tears were both a result of the reality of my wife's cancer (Chemo starts tomorrow) and the truth that God is faithful and walking with us.

There is a fair amount of grief involved. Heidi's battle with cancer will be hard on her and on our family. While her long-term prognosis is good, we still have to get through the summer. There are things I know to expect – loss of Heidi's hair, a huge financial bill, summer activities to give up, and regular trips to the hospital. Other things remain a mystery – how will Heidi react to the chemo treatments? What side effects will she experience? Will the drugs be effective in relieving her discomfort? How fatigued will she be? How will the kids react as her health deteriorates and she loses her hair? Etc.

Whatever the answers to those questions are, one thing is certain: we have a long road ahead of us. And so all of this sort of caught up with me this afternoon: The painful reality of what is ahead and the joyful reality of a God who loves and cares for Heidi and my kids and me more than I can fathom; The fear of the future and the confidence of hope in the Lord; the grief of watching my wife suffer, and the comfort of the One who suffered for us.

Lord, I thank you that we do not travel this road alone. I thank you for your unfailing love toward us. I thank you for your sustaining grace. You are showing yourself faithful and I praise you!

2

Chemo Begins

Up to this point, we've just been anticipating treatment. The beginning of Chemotherapy treatments marks a new phase of our journey and brings new opportunities to trust and follow the Lord...

March 22, 2013

Round one of Chemo has begun, yesterday was long but it won't always be that long. They spent time going over all the medications for me to take plus all the Chemo's- what they are, how they work and what can be expected as side effects. So, lots of information.

The first start of the day was port access. I watched a YouTube video of how to get special cream from your Nurse and then how to apply it the right way and supposedly you will feel nothing. Well, I didn't believe it, but now I do!!! It was amazing, took my deep breath in and - Nothing! Fabulous, for me that was the worst part, now I know what to expect. Our chemo nurse is young and we found out she is a Christian, she said we can ask for her each time, and I know Todd will :) so we will be in good hands. She was kind, great and thorough!

All the medications make me wonder how I will feel but today is good. I'm weak and my body knows it has tons of meds in it, but that's okay, better than nausea and vomiting! Right? I ate some oatmeal today and half a ham and cheese sandwich and snacking on crackers and fluids! So far, so good! So, thankful for all the prayers, meals, childcare, cards, notes and phone calls, I like them! don't hesitate to call, I just won't answer if I don't want to talk :) or I'm resting, no worries!

I slept okay last night, had a few minor issues so just stayed in bed a few extra hours today. I am finally comfortable in my bed again. My port is almost all the way healed and finally today I think my hip discomfort is going away! Yeah! God is good! My regular nurse is a pure optimist :) She keep saying I'm going to sail through and Todd and I keep looking at her like, really? I think what she is trying to tell us, is they have made many advancements in cancer treatment and most people don't get sick anymore. She wants us to know they are committed to making everything the best they can.

Fatigue will be my worst enemy. The medications all will begin to overlap as they kill the cells and I will get increasingly weak. So, pray I will still have an appetite, food will help a lot, that my iron will not drop too low, it's already low. That I will stay free of sickness and infection, a big concern! Many challenges await as far as maintaining energy which will allow me to keep going, with rest as well :)

We have many things going on this year and we know that God is walking before us, we see Him working all around us, and in the people that we work for and alongside! We are so very thankful! He is providing and will continue, this we know. Pray for continued strength. Todd is moving part of his office and library home, so he can be here for summer and available. Many changes but we are also thankful that this is just a part of the journey and in time I will heal and be healed! Have a blessed day!

March 25, 2013

So, Sunday was long and exhausting but good. I was thankful to be able to make it to church. After church we had a ground breaking ceremony for our Church, we plan to see the building going up the first week of June! After that I had lunch with my parents, I was thankful they were able to come for the day and finished the afternoon off watching Ashley in her final performance of Cinderella. I returned home around 7 and went fast to sleep.

Today has been mostly rest, I plan to spend most of my days resting and have the energy to spend the evening with Todd and the kids. I know we will find a new normal. Days talking, instead of being busy and going non-stop. Lots of movie time and sharing time.

Most of my fog has lifted due to the medications I only have to take 3 days after my Chemo, that is good. However, I have a lot of concerns about my physical strength. I am already a bit anemic and chemo will add to that. We are discussing diet and making sure I'm getting enough calories, hard to balance everything. As of last night my tongue feels like it's on fire, thankful for no mouth sores and would appreciate prayers that this will be a temporary issue. Even drinking water and all food, causes burning. So, one day at a time, still.

I am anticipating feeling a bit stronger tomorrow and very thankful for chemo only being every 2 weeks! A little time to rebuild strength. Thank you all for your continued prayers, notes, visits and food. It all is a huge blessing! Heidi

March 27, 2013

It's Wednesday and it's been a long week so far. Reality is hitting a bit too hard for me. I think I continue to ask and think about what will a new normal be...

I had anticipated feeling much better, I seem to be in a fog, the way you feel when really sleepy or if you have taken some medication. The problem is I'm not sleepy and on no medication. My brain doesn't seem to be "thinking clearly". I'm struggling with, will this be my new norm? If I'm sitting, I know I don't feel well but when I get up I know it all the more clearly. Life seems to be in a slow motion. The thought of doing the daily normals is fading, the question of how then will they get done, if I can't do them continues. A really helpless feeling inside. Here me, I know we have support and will figure this out, but how do you let go so fast? It's hard to accept it all at once when it's happening and you have no control.

I had thought I would just rest, read, watch a movie, listen to things, I am doing some of that, but it's like I'm over stimulated very easily. I really don't have the stamina to do a lot of that. I'm thinking if this is how I feel now, what do the months ahead hold. How much will I miss? There are just so many feelings and emotions I'm not sure how to deal with. Crying seems to be a part of life now, things just hit you, realities. YouTube is a great thing, listening to others stories and getting information but every time I see a bald person, reality hits again. How will this be me? How is this my life? This will be my new normal, our family's new normal. Sickness for a time.

I thought I did well at the one day at a time thing... I really think I had no idea. Moment by moment right now, moment by moment. Each day, different than the one before. God will walk us through each and every moment but some moments I'm not sure how... it's so much harder than I realized it would be and we are just beginning. Thank you for your love and prayers and encouragement! I know that in the end we will only have gotten through because of God and all those He has placed in our lives to pull us through!

March 28, 2013

Today the sun is shining and I'm so happy! After a rough 2 days, things began to get better last night, the fog began to lift and I was able to think a bit more clearly! It was like I didn't want to get excited because I wasn't sure if I would stay that way. As I awoke this morning, I feel okay! I will take okay, not fabulous but rested and able to think a bit more! Thank you all for your prayers. I was also having port pain yesterday and today it seems to be gone. I'm beginning to realize each day will be different, different challenges, different aches and pains.

Last night I was able to go into the library and get a movie for Kate and I felt almost normal, it was great, then we stopped and grabbed some candy for her to fill eggs, I think she is planning her own egg hunt for Sunday :) I've been a bit behind. Can't believe we are looking at April, Easter, Spring break, where are the days going...

I'm thankful for today and all the wonderful people God has placed around us. For a wonderful, loving and completely committed husband. I am blessed and daily reminded to live today! I am still struggling with all that will be lost this summer, things we want and planned to do, but God will care for those things and make something beautiful even from our disappointments, I have to believe that.

Today I go to a wig consultation, Kaitlin is going with me and excited :) Todd wants to come too so we will all go together. Tomorrow I will cut my hair, not sure we are ready but one step at a time. Many emotions tied to hair. We think how we look, is who we are... I know I do... we know it's not true but it's hard to separate... Well, anyway, enjoy the sunshine today, I hope it's here to stay!

March 31, 2013

Happy Easter! Today has been a good day, again! Very thankful. I was able to go to church and although tired and worn out, it was good to be there with friends and family. We grilled out for lunch, Kate colored eggs, and then we had an egg/candy hunt in the back yard, just for fun.

So, Thursday I was not feeling great but made it to my appointment for a wig. The ladies were great and very helpful. I was glad that Todd went with me. On Friday I went to get my hair cut, I really didn't care about getting my hair cut but was not feeling all that well when I arrived. I was so thankful for the friend who cut my hair, cut my wig (the one given to me) and was just kind, helpful and didn't charge me a penny. She made the whole experience as easy as it could have been. I then over did by going to the grocery store with the girls and was thankful to just make it back home.

The kids are beginning to see my limits and I think that is making the process of pitching in and helping much easier for them. They have had breaks and gone to friends, so that has been helpful.

As I'm looking at Chemo once again on Thursday, I'm really trying not to think about it! Hoping Monday- Wednesday will be fairly normal around here. Spring Break, Dentist appointments, a friend visiting and Max will turn 13! I'm very thankful that many bad days came and went, it was hard when they came but when they went it made me realize that no one day is the norm. I feel like I know a bit more what to expect with round 2, basically 8 days of yuck and mess and then a few good days! But hey, there were good days, so that is what I will focus on!

Thankful for all those praying and encouraging and small gifts to let me know I'm thought of... overall it's been rough and emotional, this past week and I know there are moments ahead I'm still not looking forward to but I know we will get through them together! I'm not alone and I have many loving and caring for me! God is good! Have a great week, I plan to, at least the first half! Heidi

April 2, 2013

Today was a long day - full! Full of kids, running, crying, shopping, so much! I'm thankful for one more day before the next Chemo. Tomorrow is Max's 13th Birthday.

Today, I felt emotions up and down, I rested but could not sleep as I processed so much. Reality of life is tough... today we had to tell our 13-year old daughter that her friend from school was killed this last week, his name just being released last night. The pain, and grief. The reality that 6 blocks from my house a young man made a horrible decision to shoot bullets into a house full of a family taking the life of one of the children. Needless suffering and pain.

Today I received a gift from a child who I have never met. A child who knows my son. She asked for prayers for ME! at her church, she made a blanket for ME and gave it to Max with a note stating they were praying for ME. Wow... a child I have never met.

Today as I drove the kids home from the mall, some kids were walking outside and we recognized one of the girls. This particular girl shaved her head last week for a cause! Her cousin died from cancer just a few months ago and she raised $1,000 and shaved her head. I saw her bald head from the car. We stopped and rolled down the windows and she ran over and hugged Me! An amazing thing to me... her courage to take a radical stand, she is brave and a beautiful little girl! She pulled out her Orange hat that said - Cancer sucks! she asked me if I wanted one! I told her I agreed with her hat!

> We can't fix the pain but we can continue, knowing that someday, if we are God's children... it will come to an end and I know who wins!!!

I am just amazed at the amount of pain and struggles that our children face each day, yet some rise above and some make decisions in the moment that change their lives and the lives of others forever! Our world is tough and I know without the hope that someday all pain and suffering and sin - itself will be gone forever... I know I couldn't handle it. I am thankful for a God who yes, for a time, allows sin on this earth but I know that He never loses control. In the end He will be the victor! He has conquered sin and death and only through Him do we have hope! This life is hard, but we press on, we fight, we teach our children the truth, we teach them who God is... we don't have all the answers, we can't fix the pain but we can continue, knowing that someday, if we are God's children... it will come to an end and I know who wins!!! Thankful always for each day and for the young children who make choices to stand strong, to know who they are... our lives touch those around us, don't think they don't. We all want to be loved and accepted... God loves and accepts us as we are and changes us, so thankful... Thankful he covers my sin, I will never be perfect but He is... He accepts me how I am... flawed. So, much to process, so much to be thankful for... One more good day tomorrow, thankful... Heidi

April 4, 2013 – Deleted (Todd)

Note: These thoughts were posted on CaringBridge, then immediately deleted. As a pastor, I felt it was too much to air at that moment, but the post is included here. Even when there is loving support of Christian Community, it's easy to feel overwhelmed and alone. Even when you know others love and care about you, even when you feel close to others, it doesn't always feel "safe" to share what is really going on with you emotionally and spiritually.

Well, today we head to Chicago for the second chemo treatment. The past two weeks have been tough with many ups and downs both physically and emotionally. Not sure yet what the normal patterns of struggle will be or what all will happen before these months are through. One of the biggest blessings is having supporting friends and family to encourage, pray, and help in practical ways. The outpouring of support toward us has been truly amazing and we appreciate it greatly.

Ironically, one of the struggles is that even in the midst of all this support, I still feel alone. Some of the things I am feeling I cannot articulate and even when I can, there is no one to share them with. I am uncomfortable with my own feelings and it seems I just have to feel them alone. No one seems to be the right audience – friends, family, peers, even Heidi. When I try to put my feelings into words, the hearer either can't comprehend or can't handle what I have to say, so for the most part I just keep silent. Granted, the emotions I have surrounding all that is happening might be irrational or even sinful, but I need to speak them and I guess the Lord is the only one who can handle hearing what I have to say.

And so that's the paradox that is my life right now – never have I felt more supported and never have I felt more alone.

April 5, 2013

So, Chemo days are not bad in and of themselves. I feel no stress going and the process is a bit long but easy. I am able to eat and do whatever I want and Todd is there right beside me. We even hit very little Chicago traffic yesterday which is amazing since we left at 5:30, so thankful for that.

The effects began to hit me in the middle of the night. Night sweats have begun. I did not have them before Chemo. The Dr. said it is "good" indicating that the cancer cells have been found and the chemo is attacking them. My Iron counts were the same as last week, so that was good, they had not dropped. I feel basically the first 8 days will be a struggle to eat and drink what I would normally and so I drop some weight and strength and then the last 5 days, I'm hungry and I eat all I can to regain strength. I feel more prepared food wise and mentally for the next week. I am even going to shower before my next round of Meds so I won't be druggy, last round showering was even difficult at first, so figuring out even the basics.

Lastly, my white cell counts are very low. In any other kind of chemo, they would stop until they came up and then continue. However, they explained that even though mine are very low and I need to be VERY careful about infections, with Lymphoma it's different. My counts will drop before chemo (that's when they do the blood work) and then the week after they do come back up. It's just something they have learned over the years. So, they do not stop treatment for low white cell counts unless I would get really sick. Infection is a big concern but again, those who have MY type of cancer tend to get less infections than other types of cancers.

So, we continue to learn all types of things. I did ask about foods and my Dr. said eat whatever makes you happy. Getting rid of the cancer at this point is our goal and we just want you to hang tight, be as strong as you can and eat whatever you want and can! I like that! I'm a pretty healthy eater, anyway... no comments :) Who doesn't like cookies, chocolate, cake, cheesecake... well, you get my point!

The good news is that the Dr. was able to really look at all my scans and has concluded that what had originally been a possibility of a mass on my lung actually is just showing that the large lymph node in my chest wall is just pressing on the lung. There appears to me no additional mass. Praise God! He stated that my PET scan will be done after 4 rounds (that is 4 months) and he expects it will be clean! then they still do two additional rounds before ending Chemo. So, always lots of information but today I feel good so far, haven't gotten out of bed but doing okay in bed :) Kids last day of Spring Break so we will have some time together! and Ashley is off to Grace College with a friend to hang out and visit for the weekend. I'm thankful they are able to just continue on and do fun things.

> We are not alone, He walks each step with us, some days He is carrying me and carrying you!

Thanks for continued prayers. On my dresser I have two wigs sitting, Ashley says it's creepy :) so we will have many more emotional days ahead in the next few weeks, but I'm thankful to have had time to process and prepare. Just continued prayers for Todd and the kids, in a way it's harder on them to watch and have to pick up all my slack :) thankful for the days I can do stuff but they are limited. Well, I've gone on and on and still thinking of more I wanted to say, maybe another entry later about life and expectations... tough subject but much food for thought! Thankful! Heidi

April 8, 2013

So, this round has been a bit better. I felt well on Friday and Saturday and Sunday a bit tired, but at least able to get out a few hours. Today I slept 'til 11, amazing how I can sleep so long, strange, like my body is just lifeless and relaxed and could just sleep all day. Today my mouth is a bit funky but not as bad as last round, just hard to drink, nothing tastes quite right. I have not experienced what was to be called "chemo brain" like I did last round so I'm very excited about that. I skipped my anti-nausea medications yesterday because I didn't need them so that was good as well.

This week I will likely lose my hair, it started thinning a bit yesterday. I'm not too bothered by it yet, amazing how much hair you really have on your head. I know cutting it will be rough and sad for all of us and the days are numbered, I think we all kinda hoped I might be the one person who doesn't actually lose their hair but don't think so...

Today I called Max at school because I needed to talk to him, asked how his day was going and he said he was sad I'm losing my hair, then I asked how school was due to the death of the student last week. He went on to tell me that the family was able to donate his heart and many other organs and save the lives of many. It just breaks your heart to see such loss and then see what good can come from pain. The fact that my children are dealing with all this is so very hard. Life is hard. Our hope and all expectations are from God and Him alone! He alone is our salvation! May we be able to point others to Christ, midst our pain and the reality that this life is just for a moment... enjoy today, love today, today is all we are guaranteed! In this life there will be trouble, but Jesus has overcome! Praise God!

April 10, 2013

So, tonight I have many thoughts after a long day but one weighs heavy on my heart. A young girl I have met through FB, we are on the same journey, she is one week behind me. She is discouraged and struggling and tonight getting a fever and possibly looking at an ER visit. I'm so sad for her, I feel her pain and struggle. I am praying for her and ask that y'all pray for her as well! God always gives us opportunities to look outside of ourselves and pray and support others no matter who you are or what you are going through! Thanks for the prayers I know you will send for her and for all our prayers, cards, a book I received this week! Everyone is so amazing! God has blessed us so greatly.

So, today was a bit of a frustration. I think the rain brought aching in my port and additional physical aches, my Nurse says should be expected due to my white blood cell count being low. Not sure I understand it all but I get that aching could become part of my norm. So I have come through yet another day and I'm just so thankful! I think it's possible to be frustrated and thankful all the same time, good thing :) I was able to make some soup today and go to the store... it's all good. Just so strange to go from going all the time to lucky if I can go for 1-2 hours a day. Life has truly changed.

Today I had some of those moments again, where I ask, should I actually be thinking these things... like... anyone who has eaten at my house since I've had very long hair, usually finds some hair in their food. I know... gross! Well, it's normal around here. So, today after my shower, I thought - Yikes! no one should eat at our house today... there was hair everywhere! All over my clothes, just keeps falling. Really is amazing how much hair you actually have on your head though... I think it will last 'til Sunday! We shall see... if not I will be getting another super short cut.

I found a really cute hat yesterday on a very short trip to the mall. Kaitlin found a Huge Pink Sun hat, about 3 times the size of her head, that she really liked - she looked fabulous! For those who know Kaitlin - you can picture this :) So, I also found some bandana's yesterday around the house and tried them on... trying to get used to the idea of no hair. I mean really - how do you get used to that idea? I don't believe anyone looks in the mirror and wonders - what will I look like without hair? Maybe you have. Even when I thought - I might have cancer, it was still a strange idea. I was also dealing again today with the idea of having cancer, Me! I don't feel great honestly, but the idea of having cancer still seems very unreal! It's a big thing... a big deal... me cancer? Crazy! So back to the reality that I think not having to do my hair all summer might be something I can get used to. I guess I will have to take a few pictures of my brother and I, I joking told him, I really didn't want to be his twin, but life is funny sometimes. I realize right now that one day something is funny to me and the next emotional part of the process I guess.

So, tomorrow will hold another whole set of challenges. I am reminded each day of God's care and that I am so blessed. Although this is a tough time for sure, I am so thankful... God brings us through seasons of life... *Find rest, O my soul, in God alone; my hope comes from him. He alone is my rock and my salvation; he is my fortress, I will not be shaken.* Psalm 62:5-6

A song came on the radio, I remember hearing a few years ago, in different tough circumstances... When the path is daunting, every step exhausting, You're Not alone, You're not alone![5] We are not alone, He walks each step with us, some days He is carrying me and carrying you!

April 15, 2013

Just a quick update as we start a new week. I'm thankful I started feeling better on Friday and had a great weekend. I was able to make it through all of Sunday without a nap and felt good. Church was a great as we sang a favorite song of mine right now called "Still."[6]

Hide me now under your wings,
cover me within your mighty hand....

When the oceans rise and thunders roar,
I will soar with you above the storm,
Father You are King over the flood,
I will be still and know you are God

Find rest my soul in Christ alone
Know His power in quietness and trust...

When the oceans rise and thunders roar,
I will soar with You above the storm,
Father You are King over the flood,
I will be still and know you are God

I couldn't get through this song, the words are so real to me right now, tears streamed down my face and I just enjoyed being in the presence of a loving God! He is with us, always! No matter what comes...

So, I look forward to the next few days, my good days :) Thursday will come to fast but each time it comes we get to mark one more off the calendar! God is good and this week He answered a prayer of our family that we have been praying for, for almost 2 years, never quit trusting Him! He does things in His timing and we don't always understand it but we can trust it!

As for my hair, still thinning but a hat looks better than bald, so for now I'm waiting for the next cut... not sure... we will see what the week holds... Thanks for continued prayers and support, we could not do this without you! Heidi

April 16, 2013

Today I washed and blew dry my hair for the last time for a long time. I have decided to cut my hair tomorrow. Todd and I will go together at 11:00 on Wednesday, a friend is kind enough to do it for me. I haven't given it much thought today, have kept busy, shopped for Birthday gifts all day and made Chocolate Chip cookies with Kate, I felt great all day!

So, thankful for these good days! Also, always thankful for your prayers, especially tomorrow, for both Todd and I. Chemo on Thursday, you can pray that maybe a few of my rough days are due to some of my medications. My nurse is willing to tweak them a bit and see if doing that makes me feel a bit better! I'm hopeful, but the icky days are most likely from the chemo itself. No matter what this round was much better and I'm thankful to now kinda know what to expect. Basically 8 days still of resting and only having a few hours of energy but then I get 5 good days, I will take that! So thankful for all of you!!!! Heidi.

April 17, 2013

So, we did it! I made the appointment and went to my friends and let her cut my hair! Tensions were high and I was a bit emotional on the drive over, but I knew inside it was time to just do it! God places people in our lives and I'm thankful for the friend He has placed in my life to cut my hair. May seem small but today it was not!!! Had I gone anywhere else or had Todd done it, it would have just been buzzed BUT today was different.

She started in the back, moving slowly forward! She loves cutting hair so she was having fun, and she was "trying" different haircuts! One was like a punk rocker! I felt I needed a pink strip down the front of my bangs :) We stopped when we got to the top and she ended up leaving it with just enough to spike, so I'm not completely bald, but anticipate after Chemo tomorrow, the days will be numbered before it's all gone. The transition is good. After mention of the pink strip, we ended up having fun and using the spray we had at home, it was purple, and had a little fun. If you don't have FB then Todd will eventually post pictures on here. Kate came home from school and just giggled and rubbed my head! Ash and Bailey are coming now, we will see what they say... Bailey will likely scream! Ashley, will probably think it's crazy! I will pick Max up from Football and he too... well who knows.

The fact is I'm so thankful God has given us the grace to have fun... My friend also cut my wig and it looks great, like my real hair, so I have options. No one in Merrillville will know who I am this summer based on my hair/hat/no hair choice for the day but oh well... life is what we make it, right? God is good! I feel good today and I have much to be thankful for...

Todd and I then went out to lunch, with my wig on, not my purple hair, no worries! and a short trip to the mall and then I also picked up a free halo hair piece to wear under all my cute hats! another free program, how wonderful! A great day, when we had been dreading it for a long time! Again, God is good and He has been very busy counting the hairs on my head lately! He even cares about the hairs on our heads! A good God!

Chemo again tomorrow, one more down and going to miss feeling good for another week... but on we go... Heidi

April 19, 2013

So, I will start with my funny story and then all the details for those who want them...

Yesterday, was really the first day I really acknowledged at a different level that I have cancer. Looking in the mirror at yourself with a hat and ears :) and your smile and no hair is a strange thing. My brain kept reminding me, Yes, Heidi you do have cancer. I know that at the moment you feel good but you really are sick... stupid brain. Anyway, so for our trip yesterday I decided to just wear my hat, long day... so wanted to be comfortable.

So, I fast forward to the end of our trip, we had left Chicago and stopped at McD's to grab Todd some food, upon entering there was a group of older folks kinda standing by the door, probably saying their goodbyes and blocking the way to the bathroom, so I said excuse me, smiled and walked between them. Then there is that moment when they look at you and smile and you feel like they are thinking, Oh, poor girl, she has cancer, so young! don't look and smile for too long because it would be impolite :) So I just smiled back and proceeded on. As I got into the bathroom and saw myself again, I just smiled! I think it's stranger for others to see me all the time, I only look in the mirror a few times a day. So, I leave the bathroom and again have to walk through them and they smile again. As we are leaving a man opens the door and is overly polite :) As I got outside I just laughed out loud, kinda funny. I have always been the person who does not like attention drawn to me, so this is a whole new dynamic. People look at you different when you are sick, so I will keep smiling!

> I'm so thankful God has given us the grace to have fun!

I am thankful for my wigs, though. I wore hair to school yesterday and today as to not horrify my children who have not told all their friends and it's nice to look in the mirror and have a bit of normalcy. I also told Todd that with the wind and crazy weather I anticipate one of my - most embarrassing moments coming in the near future... wig flying off my head when not expecting it!

So, yesterday was full of blessings! The worst part, we sat for 3 full hours in the car going about 20 miles maybe, not sure. The road we got on was flooded, at the end, so for over 3 hours we sat in the car as 3/4 lanes merged into one to cross a path of the road that was flooded. So, 4 hours in the car and we arrived safely at the hospital. I was so thankful for safe travel, the fact that we did not have children with us! My nurse who planned and pushed my blood work through so we could get Chemo!!!! If they hadn't accommodated us, I could have had to wait almost another week for treatment, they were booked! God is good, we were there 'til close but we got treatment!

Oh, another funny story from yesterday, Todd has a few shirts he likes to wear, One I bought says - I love my wife. That's it, I got it for him for Christmas and made him open it and put it on before giving him the best Christmas gift ever - A new Martian Guitar! Todd loves to play guitar and has never had a nice one, so I saved and saved and gave it to him...

So, he wore that shirt to my first Chemo and the nurses loved it! Yesterday, he wore a new t-shirt he ordered, says - No one fights alone and one of the lines is in purple for Hodgkin's Lymphoma. As our nurse came to our cubby, she said, - I love your shirt, a few weeks ago there was this couple and the wife bought him a special guitar for Christmas and a shirt that said, - I love my wife! We just laughed and said, yeah, that is us! So, when you think people don't talk about others, they do :) Keep it good! So, I guess everyone is not crazy and supportive like us! Thankful for an amazing husband, I am not annoyed by his t-shirts and support in a quiet way :) No announcements or gathering on my behalf or needing to shave your head for me, please but t-shirts are good :) He has ordered matching t-shirts for the whole family so be watching for a picture... On that note, look at the pictures above, he did post the hair cutting!

So, today I feel good, always afraid the days after chemo to get out of bed, sometimes in bed I feel fine but moving and walking are not the best. Today, however I was able to get up and eat and manage going to the school to see Kate in her poetry recital. I was very proactive to eat much and care for myself last round and it had paid off... My blood work was good yesterday, white count was higher (although still really low, but improved) and my hemoglobin was higher than last round too! I even weighed in 3 lbs more! Yeah! Funny how we worry about our weight and hair and now I'm without hair and excited that I've gained weight! Just so many moments that are insane! So, I felt cruddy during chemo, could feel the medications sinking in but last night I really felt well once we got home! Praise God...

So, praying for continued strength as chemo continues, I am likely to get more tired but so far so good. I feel I have always been good about knowing my limits. Also, I have had this brain fog I have complained about and wished would go away, it has only been a few days each round but frustrating. As I was working hard to articulate exactly what I feel, my nurse listened intently and did some research. She found out that one of my anti-nausea pre- meds showed in studies that 17.8 % of patients have the complaint I have. She stated she has not ever had a patient with this specific complaint. She contacted a colleague and asked advice and they suggested she pull the pre-med. So, Saturday is usually when this side effect hits so I have to wait 'til tomorrow to see if that was the issue, but I'm hopeful. I was nervous giving up that med in fear of getting sick last night but I just took a different med and I'm feeling okay today. Eating and drinking much to stay strong and amazed that despite all the icky and yucky of Cancer, I think I'm doing amazingly well! Only can be thankful! So today I am in bed, resting because I know my body needs it! I know this is long but lots going on in my head... thanks for caring and listening. May you have an amazing day, reminded that you are very blessed and God is always good!!!! Heidi

April 23, 2013

Just a quick update... I will have to say that this round of chemo has been the best. Now, yesterday and today I don't feel my best but I do feel better than the last two rounds. My hair is still an adjustment... thinning slowly still but still have some.

I was able to go to church on Sunday and manage lunch and even making cookies with Kate. I did however pay the price for that yesterday. I felt like I could have stayed in bed all day with my eyes closed and never have gotten up. Of, course that did not happen. I was able to get laundry and dishes done. I was able to sit outside and enjoy the sunshine! My brain fog never came, for which I am so thankful and my icky mouth really hasn't come this round either. Quite dry and not really excited about food today but better... So, I'm thankful that with more knowledge and a great nurse, I have been able to manage the side effects of all my medications.

I will ask for prayers for this weekend. Todd and I will be heading to a Pastor's/Wives Retreat. We are thankful that we are able to go and for all those keeping our children. Please pray that I will feel well and we would just have a refreshing, restful time away! Thanks, Heidi

April 28, 2013

So, tomorrow another week starts. Where do they go? I sometimes think if any season of life, I want to fly by, I think this is a good one. I feel it will be over fast and we will be able to look back and praise God for bringing us through!

As for today though... we had a great weekend, Thank you all for praying. We are blessed with amazing church family, so our kids were well cared for while we were gone and everyone had a great weekend. Todd and I enjoyed time alone and with many friends, visiting and catching up. Spoke with so many who have been and are praying, it's an amazing thing. Also, thankful I got to stop and visit with my sister and her family. We ate well, all weekend. I gained almost all my weight back this weekend, I've been doing such a good job at making myself eat, I'm beginning to wonder if I might gain weight while having cancer. Food is energy so I just keep eating when I can. I did come home completely exhausted but it was a great weekend!

I am a bit concerned that I seem to have a runny nose, although I'm believing that is a result of less nose hair :) Who would have thought we needed all our nose hair to keep our nose from running. However, my nose seems stuffy at times too, so I will be resting tomorrow to make sure I am not getting a cold. Friends have assured me they have been feeling the same way and think it's just the weather around here. So, prayers to stay healthy and not get a cold! Need my white cells to stay stable. Chemo will be on Thursday again, it comes so quickly. I am thrilled this has been my best round, I feel we have conquered all side effects the best we are going to be able to, so that is a huge praise, we will just keep doing what we are doing.

Was an interesting hair weekend as well. I decided to not wear my wig this weekend while away. Seems as though my kids are often the ones uncomfortable with my super short hair, yes, there is still some on my head. So, for the weekend I went without, for church I wore my wig and for those who are on FB I wore a hot pink wig for church tonight, mind you, we only have Awana on Sunday nights! We also just got all matching t-shirts, that say - No One Fights Alone - for Todd and I and all the kids! I really like them. Thankful for my husband and children! Well, time to sleep! Night all - have a great week! Thanks for reading, praying and all your comments! We are thankful!

May 5, 2013

So, it's Sunday and I had chemo on Thursday. I had been lazy in updating because I was doing really well, you will be happy to hear. My chemo on Thursday was without traffic, Yeah! we got there and in quickly and the day ran smooth. I did have to wait to see a Dr. which frustrated me because we were done early and I just wanted to be home. Nonetheless, we got home earlier than we have in past weeks and I even felt well that evening. I rested on Friday and Saturday I was able to enjoy the sunshine and some cleaning in the garage etc. Today, I was able to go to Sunday School, in addition to church service and now I'm home resting, updating since I had two people mention I hadn't updated my CaringBridge. So, thank you all for reading and continuing to pray! We strongly believe the prayers are working. My white cell counts were higher this week and my weight and Iron levels have maintained! Praise God! My hair continues to thin each day but still have a little bit on top for around the house and sometimes around town, if I'm lazy. I've discovered it's easier to manage in the convertible! So, each day, I have a new look. Some days you just need hair, so yesterday and today I enjoyed my long hair and tonight I might go with my short and a hat for church.

> Look outside yourself, love others and pray for others! God can and will use you, if you are just willing.

Well, I just feel continually blessed! I feel like the journey is not easy but easier, at this point, than we could have imagined. We are loved and supported and as I look around God is at work all around us. I believe in the days to come He is up to Big things, He will use all things and in the end He will get the glory. We must continue to love and support one another in the way God calls us to. There are so many lost and hurting people all around you and if you don't know any, then dare I say, you aren't looking. So, this week look outside yourself, love others and pray for others! God can and will use you, if you are just willing. Have a blessed week! Heidi

May 13, 2013

So, I realize I have been a bit lazy or maybe just distracted and haven't updated. I will try to do better.

Last week was actually a bit rough in a way. Just seemed really long, I was tired a lot and just didn't feel myself. I know the chemo is sufficiently confusing my body so that is part of the problem, hopefully my nurse will have solution for another minor bump in the road. I think I just need strength for the journey. Mental and emotional strength as well as physical. I find myself often being strong and just moving forward and then one day all the emotions just hit! I am not typically an emotional person so I really dislike these days :)

Midst the struggle there is always so much God is doing and teaching, seems to never end. We have seen God answer prayers as a family and for that I'm thankful. We have a very busy summer ahead of us. Our church broke ground this past week and will Lord willing lay the foundation this week! So this summer we are building a building. Looking ahead to the children being home is always mixed emotions, thankful to see them more but knowing - I must have a plan :) Looking at a few things to keep them busy, a job or one and volunteer job for another... lots of play and lots of talking :) and growing time! Todd and I have been talking about a vacation in the Fall, after Chemo ends, thinking about the end is a great thing!!!

This week will be chemo Number 5, 7 more to go! I will ask for prayers in regards to "how I feel". Seems as though I am beginning to have a bit of mental aversion to the chemo/hospital/medication etc. Not sure I can really explain this but when I start to think - Oh, chemo is coming... I get this sick feeling. Or when I see a hospital on TV or something associated... again, that sick feeling. It's a strange thing... I get it after I get to chemo too... just being there brings on this icky feeling. So, praying this week my counts will be up, I am trying to keep them there, but eating seems to have been more of a challenge this past round. Mother's Day, however, I think I ate enough food at lunch for 3 days! So that was good!

So, as always, despite the ups and downs of life, I am thankful for an amazing husband who I know would do anything for me and is a great and patient support to me! Thankful for my children... God has blessed us in many ways! Thankful for family and friends and all your prayers, we could not do this alone!

50

Oh, we will be traveling this weekend! Please pray that I will be able to manage the 2-day trip home, we are going home for a wedding and I plan on taking it very easy, no worries, but still will be a lot right after chemo on Thurs! Thanks again! Heidi

May 13, 2013

Added a new photo for those not on Face Book. Family photo - No one fights alone!

May 17, 2013

So, I got distracted but I wanted to post an update before I forgot. So, today I feel okay, normal icky, tired and spending the morning in bed. I was just able to talk to a great friend for a long time which was great, however if you would pray for their family. Another car accident and the loss of a husband, some things in life we just can't understand. Please pray for strength for them during this difficult

We have been reminded of His faithfulness, we have been reminded that He is in control of ALL things! and we are reminded that only through Him we have the hope to continue on in this world!

So, Chemo days are beginning to be a bit more of a struggle for me. After feeling as normal as normal can be for several days, it's a real downer to arrive at the hospital feeling one way and usually after my port is accessed and blood is drawn I start feeling a bit weird and then it continues through Chemo. I then notice after chemo my ability to handle the sun, bright lights and noise changes for several days. My tolerance is low. My counts were all good and my weight up! So that is a praise, today of course, food sounds icky so back to finding something to eat. I did take something to help me sleep last night so I'm thankful I feel rested today and slept all night. The chemo tends to make me wake up a lot, every couple hours during the night and I have to drink a lot during the night, which causes bathroom breaks :) so, last night NONE of that occurred, so I'm thankful.

We will be heading out of town in just a few short hours. We have a big weekend ahead of us so please pray I feel well and can do the parts of the weekend I've chosen to take a part in. I will be sure to put my health first, for all those who worry about these things :) Excited to see and spend time with family have not been home at all since New Year's I think, short of one day I went home to tell my family I had cancer. If you could pray for sibling unity as well, I would greatly appreciate that. With traveling and visiting it would be great if everyone would just enjoy the weekend without a bunch of drama :) Maybe I shouldn't share that, but it's the truth and I need others praying for that! So, thanks!

We have seen God do amazing things this week alone, we have been reminded of His faithfulness, we have been reminded that He is in control of ALL things! and we are reminded that only through Him we have the hope to continue on in this world! We long for a great day, someday when He returns and all the struggles of life are behind us and we share our Hope with others, so they can see that He is the reason we Live! Press on! He will guide the way, and give strength for the journey! Heidi

May 20, 2013

So, today I will spend the majority of my day in bed, doing work and resting as the breeze blows through the windows. I over did this weekend but I felt good and was so thankful to get through. Slept so very hard last night, so I'm thankful to feel rested but oh, so worn. Thankful for the warm air but no sunshine today for me is fine. The over cast day kinda matches how I feel, if you know what I mean.

A great weekend full of family and friends. Also, were blessed with some money to help pay bills, so we praise God for that. I'm confident that at the end of this year He will have cared for all our medical bills and we will not have any debt. So, thankful that he provides. We are daily reminded of his care for us and all His children. He is truly faithful and we are just thankful! I'm confident that this will be my best chemo round yet, and have hopes of getting my strength back in the next few days and then getting some more spring cleaning done :) Blessed! Heidi

May 22, 2013

So, I'm beginning to realize that each round I am ready to feel better sooner, unfortunately, it doesn't seem to be working. Life is busy and I continue to rest and recover from the weekend. I find it crazy that I am somehow able to ignore all the things I normally do and even ignore a messy house until my days turn around :) then all of a sudden the house seems a wreck and I feel a bit overwhelmed. I thought today would be my turn around day, but still feeling a bit weak, so hiding out in the bedroom away from all the work, mostly sorting and organizing, getting ready to move the house stuff around and put another wall up in the basement so the kids have more space, small bedrooms in this house but thankful for space.

Last night was like the first night of summer, kids everywhere, hanging out, neighbor mad at the kids because the ball keeps going in his yard :) Breeze blowing through the windows, friends stopping by... so much going on, it was all good, I even laid on the couch and read. With all the craziness it was a nice night, quiet, everyone content and enjoying the evening.

So prayers for strength and today I have a bit of pain, I'm waiting for it to go away. Afternoons seem to be the time I get my best part of the day and God knows I need it when all the kids come in. Hoping tomorrow will be my official turn around day :) the sooner it comes the less stuff I have to try to cram into my good days. Thankful that despite all God continues to bring blessings into our lives, He continues to remind us that He is Good and in Control, it's going to be a long summer for many reasons but in the Fall, I know the Harvest of Blessings will come and I can't wait! Heidi

May 29, 2013

So tomorrow marks Chemo #6, that means we are half way done. I believe I see the Dr. next round, so I imagine then maybe we will be doing another scan soon to see what progress is being made.

I feel like I have been a bit more tired over all this round, this however does not mean I have slowed down or have been unable to do all the normals of each day. Had a few nights I didn't sleep well, so I think that through me off a bit too. We have been sorting and cleaning and moving some furniture around, but it's done now! Yeah!

I feel like my brain gets a little more fried each time :) like I keep wanting to say things and words just aren't there. I do pointing some times and have to just pause and wait and see if the word comes to mind, sometimes it doesn't. I'm thankful for the calendar to remind me of things I need to do and what day it is :)

So, overall my inconveniences are just that, a bit of a pain, but today I was able to go to work and I was thankful for that. For those who don't know, I volunteer at our Crisis pregnancy center and really enjoy being an advocate there. This was the second day, since getting cancer, I've been able to go in and work and I really enjoy it.

So, tomorrow we head out early to chemo, Ashley has a concert tomorrow night so please pray that I will be able to make it to the concert. I plan to come home and nap and rest and then go. She has a solo!!!! and is very excited. The kids also finish school next week on the 5th and I'm a bit concerned about balancing having everyone home for the summer. Please pray for unity, and lots of patience. I get overly stimulated easy and if any of you know my children... well, enough said! God is good and will continue to. Praying for good days that we can shop, and go to the park and even the beach. I know we will have them. So, enough said, time for a brownie! Thank you all for reading and praying! Heidi

May 30, 2013

So, I'm in the hospital now and finishing up chemo, in and out in 2 1/2 hours today! That's a record and I'm excited, we will be home in no time, about the time the kids are home from school. I will rest and then we will go to Ashley's program! Thankful the day is running smooth! Thanks for the prayers and thankful for my Dad who is at my house now, building yet another wall in our basement so we can have another bedroom! We appreciate it so very much! There are no more places to build walls so our house is complete :) Well, checking out. My counts were good today, I assume, no one told me any different and now I'm beginning to think as far as my weight goes, I may gain weight during chemo by the end :) All is going very well, prayers are working! Heidi

June 3, 2013

So, today I awake, slowly, recovering from a long weekend. It's 10 a.m. and I'm just beginning to move.

Today, Todd and I celebrate 18 years of marriage. I am so thankful for a life that has been shared with someone who is like minded in life and ministry. It's been an amazing thing to watch over the years. Life has been up and down and we have traveled and grown together. I think one theme that has reoccurred in our life as a couple has been that we don't want to just live life. We don't want to just be married, have kids, have a job and money and that's it. Those are all great and important things but in the end, can we look back on our life together and say we made a difference, we lived outside of ourselves, we pointed others to Christ, we shined a light that will lead others to a faith that leads to more than this life - eternity with Christ!

In the end, can we look back on our life together and say we made a difference, we lived outside of ourselves, we pointed others to Christ, we shined a light that will lead others to a faith that leads to more than this life - eternity with Christ!

The past few days I have looked at our life and thought, what is going on? What is God doing? Oh, I know part of what He is doing because He is answering prayers and working all around and I see it, but I only see part of the picture. Each day is full and exciting and Challenging! We can't do it without Him, this we know. We can't do it alone, He has given us each other! He has given us, family, beautiful children, friends and prayer warriors all around. We are so truly blessed.

On Thursday my chemo went well and fast, then I proceeded home to a wall being built by my Dad, who took him time and energy to bless us in that way. Then we went to see our beautiful oldest daughter sing a solo and perform in her choir. It was a great and long day, but God gave me the strength. Then Friday came, I rested all morning then went on a hunt for 2 dressers on Craigslist and through that endeavor, I met a lady who encouraged me and I her. We were able to share and pray together, a stranger but united in Christ. Another man, came and delivered a dresser for me, what a blessing and that night, although tired I was able to go to Home Fellowship Group and share and pray with friends. Another great day. Saturday was full, appointments, shopping and blessings all day, I knew I would sleep well Saturday night, but no, didn't happen. My body does what it wants the first 3 days after chemo, sleep sometimes and sometimes I just lay, unable to sleep. Sunday, I slept 3 hours straight and then today just got out of bed at 10, recovering. But so much to praise God for, our hearts are full and overwhelmed.

I will ask that y'all pray for continued strength. Yes, half way there but still seems like a long rest of the journey. As the kids are home, resting will be more difficult, on some days. God is doing A LOT in the life of our family. We believe we will be bringing another teenager into our house in the next few weeks, God has opened the door WIDE and we are teaching our children that life is about following God, not our feelings. It's not about being selfish in the moment, we must love others and invest in others' lives, living outside ourselves brings the most Joy! Christ did this! What is love? My friend spoke yesterday and I liked what she said - God is more concerned about our Character than our comfort. I think we are often too comfortable with life, time to look outside of your comfort zone and invest in those around you, I promise it will not be easy, and it will not come without sacrifice but it will be so worth it and I pray that some day when we stand before Christ, He will say - Well, done good and faithful servant! We will never do it perfect but we will go out trying, seeking to be faithful, seeking to love those others choose to not love... God is good and so faithful! So, life is ever changing for us around here, we don't know what the summer holds, although I believe a bit of insanity is on the calendar:) but we must embrace life, the one God has given us, we must live it to the fullest, all it's up and downs knowing that Christ is Sovereign and in it all He chooses to use us, His beautiful creation to accomplish His will! What an amazing thing! Have a blessed day! Heidi

June 14, 2013

So, the last few weeks have been exhausting. Not necessarily from the cancer. I have been maintaining and keeping up, I feel. I do struggle with "working with half a brain". I ask frequently what day is it? and look at my calendar for many reminders of what I need to do. Having the kids home has been good but a bit more challenging.

Today, I am reminded of Galatians 6:7-10 ESV

> *Do not be deceived: God is not mocked, for whatever one sows, that will he also reap. For the one who sows to his own flesh will from the flesh reap corruption, but the one who sows to the Spirit will from the*

Spirit reap eternal life. And let us not grow weary of doing good, for in due season we will reap, if we do not give up. So then, as we have opportunity, let us do good to everyone, and especially to those who are of the household of faith.

Life is a journey- we are sowing and pouring into others' lives every moment of every day and although exhausting, worth it! When Todd and I often talk, the conversation goes to the reality that someday when we are gone or at the end of our lives we want to look back and say, - we made a difference. So, many things we invest in are not important, it's not what we have... relationships matter, loving others matters, forgiving matters, sharing Christ through all of this - the most important of all. Christ was not about Himself, He was about His Father's business... are we pointing others to Christ, are we loving the way He did?

In the next few weeks we will have 4 teens living in our house and one 8-year-old. We have been so blessed! God is always good but I don't breathe a moment right now that I don't know that He will give strength and wisdom for the journey, we cannot do it alone. What He calls us to, He equips us for... so much equipping to come. Pray for our family, for the changes, for our children to learn to live outside themselves, to be the one to show love first, it's hard even as adults and we are all limited but with Christ He will grow us all and teach us.

So, many things we invest in are not important . . . relationships matter, loving others matters, forgiving matters, sharing Christ through all of this – the most important of all.

As for my health, today I feel pretty good, the challenge comes when I get out of bed and don't always feel great. I felt extra Icky during Chemo yesterday. I was so exhausted going into Chemo, I fell asleep twice waiting for my appointment. When I got my room, I immediately thanked the nurse and God because I got a room with a bed! Usually, I'm in a little cubical and the chairs are not real conducive to taking naps, so I curled up, got a warm blanket and even had them close the door and turn off the light. I did end up with extra nausea medication because I just didn't feel quite right but by the time I got home it was better.

I saw my Dr. and he could not feel any more lymph nodes which we could once feel, so he took that as a very good sign. My PET should be on July 9th if we get the insurance approval by that date, this will be done two days before my 9th Chemo. They wait to get the full effects of 8 complete chemo treatments. They assume the scan will show negative, please pray for a negative!!!! scan. They will do 4 more treatments after regardless but if the scan shows anything we will have to address that issue. So again, praying for a clear scan and CT's.

No one mentioned anything about my blood work, so I assume it was a normal, I have not been sick, so thankful! My weight remains normal. All good stuff. On my really good days, I sometimes wonder if after all this my good days will become better than ever. I hope to begin exercising and getting more in shape and to have a renewed sense of energy. Maybe it was the cancer holding me back before, was always so tired.

> Know that when it's hard, greater things are to come — hold tight, cling to Christ, he will pull you through, and someday it will all be worth it!

So, Todd and I discuss yet again, even before ending this update. The best things in life are hard... if you want a degree you have to work hard, if you want scholarships you have to work to be the best you can be, if you want a promotion you have to... you get my point... what we choose to invest in is different for everyone but it's always hard and challenging... it makes it all the more worth it in the end... greater reward, greater joy! Invest in others, only in that will become your greatest joy, know that when it's hard, greater things are to come – hold tight, cling to Christ, he will pull you through, and someday it will all be worth it!

I think that's enough for this post. My mind goes and goes and lately with the chemo... it's going like never before but we will get through this and God will be glorified but it won't be easy. So do not get weary in doing good, what are you sowing? are you sowing? the reaping will be worth your perseverance! As God provides opportunity put all selfishness aside and do good to everyone, He will help, and the reward will be great!

Though the darkness may last for the night, the Joy comes in the morning! Thank you all for your faithful prayers... Heidi

June 24, 2013

So, much has been going on in our lives. This Sunday was one of those days you just have tears come over and over, Worship songs often, I cannot get through on Sundays, I just stand and absorb the words, reality of who God is... this week was one of those weeks.

One song said, "God, you do not faint, You don't grow weary." My immediate thought was "God, I want that, I want to not faint and grow weary!" So, much in life is causing this to occur, being tired, kids home all the time now and my not planning alone time for myself. (This week, I'm planning better) You are an amazing God! I'm thankful that you don't faint or grow weary and some day when this life is over, I too will be a new creation, I will not faint or grow weary!

Our youth led worship and service on Sunday and did an amazing job! They taught a new song and this one,[7] I couldn't even sing at all...

Sovereign in the mountain air,
Sovereign on the ocean floor,
With me in the calm, with me in the storm

Sovereign in my greatest joy,
Sovereign in my deepest cry,
With me in the dark, with me at the dawn

In Your everlasting arms, All the pieces of my life
From beginning to the end – I can trust You!

In Your never failing love You work everything for good;
God whatever comes my way I will trust You.

All my hopes, all I need, held in Your hands;
All my life, all of me, held in Your hands;
All my fears, all my dreams, held in Your hands

So, God is sovereign through all! I am so thankful. I'm thankful for all of you who continue to pray for me and our family. I'm thankful for continued cards and notes and meals. Everyone is so amazing. I'm thankful that God reminds me every day that He gave me the most wonderful partner to do life with! Without my husband who loves and cares for me and is doing all he can to make me rest and take care of myself despite all the craziness around us. Thank you Todd for all you do, I cannot do it alone! God is good.

As for my health, this round has been tiring. The kids are out of school full time and I really didn't account for the toll that would take on me physically and emotionally. So, please pray for continued strength, pray that I would plan better, plan for rest! Plan for quiet time, I now have Mom's QT on the calendar for each day, we plan everything else, this is now a must.

He is always good, and Sovereign! Never doubt only trust and when I am weary and fainting, I can fall into His arms! He is there to catch me, refresh me, hold me and pick me up and give me strength for the next moment!

Excited that this week we will hit #5 in the countdown! Feels good to see the numbers getting smaller. I should get confirmation of my scans being on July 9th. We are also traveling to my parents for just Fri/Sat to celebrate some Birthdays, like 16, grandchildren's all in one day :) A bit of insanity but will be a good time! Pray for strength and that I feel well. I usually do these first days after chemo.

> Be blessed, look for the good in the bad and rough days, it's always there if you know Christ! It's always there!

Pray for our children and Todd and I. We have much going on within our home. We do not doubt, ever, this is what God has called us to do. It has its challenges but He will always equip you for what He calls you to do, it will not be easy but it will daily remind you that You are not the one who does the work - Christ does it through you! I need His strength more and more with each moment... not day! I know summer is flying and at the end, Lord willing, I will be cancer free and we will now be a family of seven! Five kids is what we always wanted but how God has chosen to accomplish that is an amazing process.

He is always good, and Sovereign! Never doubt only trust and when I am weary and fainting, I can fall into His arms! He is there to catch me, refresh me, hold me and pick me up and give me strength for the next moment!

Be blessed, look for the good in the bad and rough days, it's always there if you know Christ! It's always there! So with tears in my eyes yet, again, because they seem to be leaking a lot :) I know God has us where He wants us! Strength for the journey and beautiful things to come! I know God is working and answering. We did have a few good days last week where I knew people were praying. Those are the moments for in that situation, the days, thank you God! that we hang on to! Growing and learning... a tough process but will be so worth it! God is good! Heidi

June 28, 2013

Today I am reminded of Isaiah 55:8-9 *"For my thoughts are not your thoughts, Nor are your ways, My ways." says the Lord. For the heavens are higher than the earth, So are My ways higher than your ways, and My thoughts than your thoughts"*

God does things His way, we will never understand that on this side of heaven. I'm convinced He allows bad things to happen or just "things" we don't want to happen now or in our ways... so that He will be the one to get the glory in the end. How we handle "the news", "the changes in life" all the circumstances that surround us, If we are Christ's children, our testimony can point others to Him. Sure we have feelings and emotions and we will not handle things perfect in the moment but where does our heart end up, does it say, I don't get it God, I don't understand Your thoughts and Your ways, but... I choose to trust You!

Reading Job, I see that His faith, His determination to follow Christ, to trust Him, even when Job was living for Christ... bad times still came, so we all ask why? why did Job have to go through all of that, Why did God allow it? Because He did. I only conclude because God knew Job! He knew Him as His child, He knew Job would be faithful, Job would testify to who God is! God would get the glory.

Jesus himself went through horrible abuse and death. Many, I'm sure sat around questioning, why? Their faith was tested... but God knew the bigger picture, Jesus had to die, so that God could accomplish much greater things. Salvation for His people! Hope for the lost! A free gift to sinners, who choose to see their sin for what it is, and accept His righteous perfect death on the cross for the payment. He did it for me! and He did it for you! Without Jesus suffering and death I could not have hope in this life. Jesus doesn't offer salvation to His people just to do it... He did it so our lives can be changed, He saves us to change us and offer us something this world never can and never will. He is all we need; this life will never satisfy. Suffering for a greater purpose! You and Me!

What is God seeking to accomplish in your life? Can you only see the pain, the struggle, or are you choosing to trust? Tough questions but we all ask them, we all wonder, well, our ways are not His! This I know and believe and will continue to believe.

A thank you for praying for our family, for unity. God has been working and continues to work and provide strength for the journey. Please continue.

Now as for my medical health. I am doing well. Chemo has been icky on chemo days, but by bedtime I am feeling okay. I slept well last night and that is a huge praise, I usually wake about every 2 hours on the first couple nights after chemo but not last night, so thankful. I need the rest because we are going home for 24 hours to visit family and celebrate Birthdays. You can pray that I can handle the stimulation, it's a lot of people and a lot of noise, no offense to all those I will be spending this time with. Happy always to see and spend time with family, just a lot. I will hide away and rest when I need to. It will all be good.

What is God seeking to accomplish in your life? Can you only see the pain, the struggle, or are you choosing to trust?

I only have 4 chemo's left and I'm ready to keep counting down. My scans are confirmed for July 9th, this will be all day, and then Chemo on the

11th, another all day thing. So pray for strength and stamina for two long days in one week, but my Birthday is on the 12th and I plan to be celebrating - No cancer detected in my body! So please pray for that for us. The months have been very long and although I am aware continually that they could have been much worse and I've been so blessed, We are ready for them to be past.

My hair... well, I'm kinda over it, most days. I usually wear a hat now. I still have a small patch of hair on top but last round it thinned a bunch more. So, I just keep thinking it's really been a blessing God left me even this little amount of hair, to make the process easier, by the end it will all be gone but then chemo will be over and it will start growing back, I'm ready. Also thankful it's summer and warm and I didn't have to endure cold with no hair. There are always blessings along the way, if we just look. For, me I have to... some days are hard and I have to realize it's all temporary, cancer (thankfully for me) and life itself. Thankful there is a great home in heaven with no more challenges, pain, suffering... There will a day with no more tears, no more pain, no more fears... thankful I know Christ and if you don't know Him in this way... He wants to know you! Have an amazing weekend, I plan to! Heidi

July 9, 2013 – "In remission" (Todd)

Heidi wanted me to post an update from her PET and CAT scans today. We just got off the phone with the doctor and he explained the results to us. Basically, in the initial scans, there were several inflamed areas, some of which were identified as Hodgkin's Lymphoma and others that were presumed to be benign. In today's scans, all of the areas that had previously been identified as cancerous are now negative for lymphoma while the other areas have either reduced or remained unchanged. We will monitor the other areas over the next couple years and/or do a further biopsy to confirm the remaining areas are benign. But, the doctor is confident enough with these scans to say the chemo-therapy treatment has worked. The bottom line, "I'm comfortable with saying that you are now in remission." Praise the Lord! The treatments have had their desired effect and there is no sign of cancer.

> There are always blessings along the way, if we just look.

In the meantime, Heidi will still have four more chemotherapy treatments over the next 8 weeks. Continue to pray for her strength as the effect of the chemo has been cumulative and the last two weeks have been the toughest so far. She is not looking forward to the remaining therapy, but we are grateful that we know that the Lord has healed her through this medical care. We continue to pray for his strength and sustaining grace even as we praise Him for this answer to prayer. Thank you for partnering with us in this.

July 10, 2013

So, I just finished watching a movie with Kate after a long day of running. So thankful to run but need the rest. I am heading into this round of chemo a little worn down, have had some physical things keeping me that way these past two weeks, always frustrating but I know the end is in sight.

So, today midst all my running had two different conversations.

One went something like this - my friend praising God for the work He has done, saying that they can't believe how I have managed cancer and all the things going on in our family and they give all the credit to God - we know it's His! I know it's His, we can't do this all alone.

My other conversation went something like this - I have been amazed to see your attitude and how you have handled your cancer, treatments and everything else, I just don't know how you have done this. My response was one word - God! Their response was that's good but I can't imagine that that would be enough... I said "He is" ... I will never fully understand this myself in this life, but I went on to say - we have no control, we have to trust Him in all things.

God is at work in us and all around us, He uses us and it's all amazing to me because at some level, most days I ask - what is today, several times... my brain is weak and I just keep going... so tired, but God knows what He is doing... In all honesty, I really don't want to get up and go to the hospital tomorrow, I really don't want to finish this all... but still I am thankful, so I press on because God is good and this is the path he has chosen for me, for us at this time. I look forward to the real end! Cancer-free is amazing and such an answer to prayer but for me it's still not over, two more months of lots to do and lots we are praying about.

Please pray for a situation with our family. God has opened doors we have prayed for, for over 2 years, and we have to wait on a court date on July 22!, 8:30 in the morning, we need the judge to say yes to a dear child, we love as our own, coming to live with us, Please pray with us, Pray for Gods will but as humans, we want God's will to match our hearts desire at this point. Thanks for your prayers and we will continue to keep you updated! Heidi

July 14, 2013

So, it's Sunday night and I have a quiet moment! Todd has taken the kids to youth and Kate went to swim at the neighbors, I don't think I have been alone in the house in about 2 weeks! That's insane. Funny how life changes. Just months ago, they were all in school and I had all day alone, I do enjoy my quiet time. Then life got crazy!

So, there is so much to be thankful for, every day I am thankful for our family. Miracles, honestly right in front of our faces. Midst the struggle and pain, there are miraculous things if we just look.

Tomorrow, Todd and our youth will leave for camp. Please pray for safety for them all. Pray that God will work in their lives. I am continually reminded that the world has so much influence on them and we are constantly fighting to teach them the truth of Who God is! Watching them grow and learn and slowing all becoming adults. A high and challenging calling in this life to raise children who love and serve the Lord! May our kids grow to Know God in a real and deep way so that when the storms of life come, and come they do... they will be armed and ready to trust!

So, I'm not feeling my best today, I realize each round that all the same strange feelings and junk come again, thankful the days are numbered. I don't sleep well on Friday night, 2-3 hours laying awake in bed, but your eyes burn so you can't just watch TV, read or do FB, basically you just get to lay tired and wait to fall asleep. Apparently sleeping meds are addictive so it's my Dr. preference that I just endure since we are close to the end and it's only one night usually. So Saturday night I slept like a rock, felt like my body weighed 300 lbs trying to drag myself out of bed for church, but I did. So tonight, just thankful for the quiet :) and a quiet week ahead, much time to think and pray, hard to find the time but thankful that when I talk to God He is right there, listening all the time, even if a kid is saying, MOM! that's about every moment anymore :) Again, just thankful for my family and a great husband to come along side me, never missing a chemo, never making me do it alone, I realize more and more each day that I can't do life alone. God has blessed me with family and amazing friends! Truly amazing, thank you all for taking this journey with us! I think in the fall I will look back and have a clearer perspective on life, right now I still feel like my brain only works half the time, but even that - God understands! He is faithful! Night all!

July 26, 2013

Psalm 37:39-40 *But the salvation of the righteous is from the Lord; He is their strength in the time of trouble. And the Lord shall help them and deliver them; He shall deliver them from the wicked, And save them, Because they trust in Him.* Psalm 37 has been a Psalm for our family this last few days, go dis our salvation, strength, help, deliverer, He will save us because we trust in Him.

We have much going on in our family besides just cancer, so many opportunities to trust... more than you will ever know. As a Christian we never finish the job of trusting God... it is always ongoing.

We thank you for your many prayers... God is at work but we must continue to trust each and every moment. Camp for our children was great. The speaker was amazing and had a real ability to share his life and story with them. God brought him out of ashes and has done something amazing in his life. So many hurting children and families and it's so important for all of us to see a walking example of God's faithfulness even in the troubles in this life. Our middle daughter whom we had been praying for had a change of heart at camp, she decided she wants to follow Christ and not this world. As we know God knows our hearts and minds, he knows when our hearts have truly been changed and we believe hers has. This in no way makes life easier right away, maybe the reality is it's just as hard, life is full of pain and temptation but the difference is the desire of the heart, the will to follow God and to know that He is always with us, every step of the way, He is on our side and in the end He wins against the pain and evil in this life, it is only temporary.

On that exciting note, God has chosen to say wait to our other situation and with the court date we attended. We know His plans are bigger than ours—the pain has been intense but He again is faithful, sovereign... He has a plan and purpose and we will fall back on the fact that WE TRUST HIM! So continue to pray for this situation for our family, we really appreciate it. Midst pain and trials we hold on tight to Gods' Word, His promises We see Him actively working all around us and on that we choose to focus.

Here is a link to an amazing song [Christ Tomlin, "Sovereign"], [8] take the time to listen... music is a great way to bring our hearts and souls to a restful place midst struggles. So we trust Him for all.

I have 2 more chemos. I basically got to sleep through yesterday's with a new medication they gave me. I requested a bed again and with the meds I got to sleep and then I slept the whole way home too... I felt decent last night, ate dinner... and right now in bed I always feel okay until I get up and moving around. I actually took half a new pill last night and slept 'til 5 a.m. woke for a short time and then slept until 9, so I was so excited!

> We know His plans are bigger than ours—the pain has been intense but He again is faithful, sovereign... He has a plan and purpose and we will fall back on the fact that WE TRUST HIM!

Sleep is always helpful, so please pray tonight goes the same, Friday nights seem to be my worst but maybe the same plan will produce the same result tonight, I sure hope so. We will be traveling to see family tomorrow for half the day, I would love to feel well for the short trip. Next week we will take a few days and head south to make some visits, again, needing strength for the journey. Keeping busy weather I feel bad or not is best, it's not that my body needs more sleep usually it just feels icky, so we just keep going 'til it passes. I actually believe it passed sooner last round, I was feeling better by Wednesday afternoon and it usually takes 'til Friday. So, less than a month and it will all be over and so will summer, 2013 has been insane but thankful for so many to walk through this journey with us, it will be a year of ups and downs that we will be sure to remember and be able later more I think to see more clearly all God has accomplished. Have a blessed Day!

July 26, 2013 – Pictures

Uploaded some new pictures for those who don't have FB, some from the beach trip we took and others from my Birthday! Enjoy!

August 9, 2013 – Life is full of ups and downs!

So, this has been a crazy month. Although I cannot share all that has been going on we are always confident that God is in control, is faithful and he is faithful to complete a good work in us, that He has begun. There has been a lot of pain and heartache this month, some adjustments and things in life just not going the way we in our humanity think they should go but bottom line as always is to trust God.

I found myself not even able to just say, hey trust God! I had to stop and think what does that really mean. I think we are tempted to say, "How? God is not trustworthy, don't you see the things happening in this world, or worse happening to me? How can I trust Him?" I have been reminded that our view of trust is different than what trusting Him really means. He promised not that life would be without pain, but that He would be there to go through the pain with us. He never promised that evil would not have its time and place in this life, He promised that in the end, He will have victory over evil, pain and the sin of this world. The perspective is never right when only focusing on the here and now, but right when we are able to try in our humanity to look to the bigger picture, the one that ONLY God can see and trust in that, trust in Him. He does have it all under control. He brings us to the end of ourselves so that all we have left is Him, His love, His salvation, His comfort, and ultimately heaven - where all this will be behind us! His plan is high and we must trust even when nothing makes sense, even if He never gives us the answers we want or think we deserve.

I look at Job, he lost family, wealth, health and God had confidence in Job's faith to know that no matter what he allowed to happen to Job, Job would be faithful. Job was not perfect, he did question, struggle, suffer, had not so great friends, who were not encouraging... as we would like. He had it rough but God had a bigger plan, I think part of the story of Job is for US! So we can see that although we don't understand it all or even deserve what is happening to us - Naked came we into this world and naked will we return, the Lord gives and takes away, blessed be His name. We place so much stock in this world. Job even went as far as to say – *"Though He slay me, yet will I trust in Him"* (Job 13:15 KJV). How is this possible? How did Job do it... I don't always know but I'm confident it can be done, he is an example. Because he was faithful, God went on to bless him in many ways.

God has been faithful to bring to mind, stories and verses, popping into my head continuously to keep me going.

As for the portion of this that pertains to my health, cancer is just part of our life and one that will hopefully be past soon. Another thing God has allowed for us to minister to others and give a voice to how great He is!

I have only 1 Chemo left! Praise God! We have chosen to put if off a few days so it will be on August 26th at 9 a.m. Ashley will turn 16 on the 23rd and we have a church picnic on the 25th so I really wanted to be at my best for these things. Especially able to plan for Ashley's B-day and enjoy dinner out with her. So I'm thankful for this adjustment, makes it all better for me :) My medication adjustments have helped, I feel pretty well today and slept good last night. I have been having nightly issues with sleeping, changes in my body from the chemo but hoping this will be short lived once we are done with the final one. Please pray that I sleep better this round. I felt way more tired last round for the full 2 weeks. My weight and all my vitals are still good. I am continually amazed that I have stayed healthy with low white blood cell counts and the amount of stress in my life. A friend said to me last week, Aren't you supposed to stay away from stress since you have cancer? I laughed and said, "have you lived my life?" I think they would have had to send me to a deserted Island alone, Hmmm? not a bad idea :) I don't think my family could live without me.

> He promised not that life would be without pain, but that He would be there to go through the pain with us.

I am thankful Todd and I were able to get away just one night, just 24 hours to be alone, it was needed, we enjoyed good weather, cool weather!

If you hate the cool summer, I think that has been a gift for me, from God. It has allowed me to be outside without worries. We also got some rest and time at the beach, we just missed getting wet with a storm blowing through but overall a perfect 24 hours. Todd also got to experience being out in public with me, with no hair. This may sound funny but people do treat me differently, look and then quickly look away (like they shouldn't stare, but then they look back anyway). For the most part I find people being kinder, holding doors for me or offering to help :) It is a real, strange dynamic. I went out last week, forgetting that I choose to wear hair that day and people were different, I realized oh - I have hair on today, they are treating me normal. Todd and I just don't go out together in the community all that much so this was a new dynamic of my cancer journey he got to see. Reality is we do stare at people who look different from us. The difference I feel for me, is most people who dress weird or whatever want the attention. I have never been a person who wants to be in the center of attention, so it's been an interesting experience.

> Don't believe the saying that people try to say comes from the Bible that "God will not give us more than we can handle" ... I believe He absolutely gives us more than we can handle at times because if we could handle it alone, WE WOULD NOT NEED - HIM!

We must look for the good in the bad and be content no matter where God has placed us. Revisited Paul speaking – *"I have learned to be content!"* (Phil 4:11). I always loved the word – "learned"! We are always learning this, new circumstances, we call "life," just keep coming at us and we constantly have to adjust and trust and choose to be content! A hard thing, but only through Christ - it is possible. Don't believe the saying that people try to say comes from the Bible that "God will not give us more than we can handle." That is not read correctly. I believe He absolutely gives us more than we can handle at times because if we could handle it alone, WE WOULD NOT NEED - HIM! He wants to be enough, He wants us to understand that all we are, every breath, every moment of the day is a gift from Him, the good and the bad because only with His help, His strength, His love... we press on... without Him, I am nothing. With Him, I have everything!

We have had many discussions about truth, know what the truth is, make sure you are believing the truth and not the "wisdom" of this world, it will lead you to even tougher times. God is truth, and His word is full of truth, even the parts we don't like! Seek Him and He promises that He will be found if we seek Him with All our heart! What is your heart focused on? A continual question that must be asked!

We love you all and thank you for reading, sorry I am not updating as much, life has been insane but looking at my September calendar it is empty! Praise God, felt good to see that, although I know that once school starts next week, it will fill. Choosing to be content in life where ever God leads us! Heidl

August 25, 2013 – Reflections from Todd on the day before her last treatment (Todd)

So, Tomorrow is Heidi's last chemo treatment – a significant milestone in our journey. Of course, we are not looking forward to it – each round has gotten progressively harder and Heidi has not fully recovered from this last round. A chemo treatment means two more weeks of sickness and exhaustion while still having to juggle home and family and a needy husband. At the same time, I am eager to get this last treatment behind us. When we leave the hospital tomorrow, what remains is recovery. In a few months our lives should return to what we call "normal." Heidi will be stronger, her hair will begin growing back, we will settle into our routines, and cancer will be a memory instead of the everyday reality it has been. Cancer has been disruptive and now that we are just getting used to dealing with it, we will be putting it behind us.

I would never wish for cancer – but I am thankful for How God has indeed worked even through cancer for our good and His glory.

Even last night, Heidi remarked how she still hadn't fully grasped the fact that she had cancer. It truly is an unreal experience. Cancer has been hard on Heidi, it's been hard on me, and hard on our family. At the same time, God has done some remarkable things in us. Now at the end, we can look back and see how God has carried us along the way – a single set of footprints in the sand.[9] Heidi and I are closer to one another than we have ever been. My relationship with the Lord has grown stronger and I am beginning to understand what it really means to depend on Him. We are to be active participants as we live our lives for the Lord, but we are not in control – He is. And we can trust Him.

So, tomorrow will be a rough day – next week will be a tough week – but we are grateful. We are nearing the end of this chapter and when things DO get back to normal, it will be a NEW normal – one that appreciates life, family, friendships and the many blessings God provides. One in which our bonds of marriage and family are stronger. One that appreciates the true beauty of our love for each other. One in which we are learning to walk with God and trust Him in everything. One in which we long for the day of His coming. I would never wish for cancer – but I am thankful for How God has indeed worked even through cancer for our good and His glory.

August 25, 2013

And the journey continues... I see Todd posted and he is always so good with words. Me, I just ramble all my thoughts... I'm tired, that is the bottom line. I have felt the effects of continued chemo and just life over the last two weeks. I am thankful that I was able to post pone my last chemo because I realize now, I never could have pulled off a surprise party for our daughters 16th Birthday just days after chemo. The party was a success and so much fun to see her enjoy friends and family and fun for her Birthday. Today, we have our annual community church picnic, again - I would have been unable to take part if I had chemo this last Thursday. I feel nothing really about tomorrow coming and going at the moment, I have found life to be too busy and stressful these last few rounds to even be able to have anxiety about the chemo itself. Today - full, tomorrow a long list of to-do's before we head to Chicago. Busy is good but busy is tiring.

True, as Todd said, I keep thinking - I had cancer? How? I really didn't have time for this :) Life just keeps going. I have found myself, feeling worn, achy, some additional pains that have come with some stress lately. Sleepless nights, I wake about every 2 hours, assuming that is effects of all the chemo. I look forward to sleeping 9 hours straight again. I have a fan by my bed, I turn it on and off all night long, depending on my body temperature. Our youngest has gotten up the last two mornings with a small jacket on :) she said, "I was so cold last night." Sorry, my fault, keep adjusting the air :)

I have no idea what Fall holds, rest I hope :) a season of rest, can't say having cancer has really been that. Lack of ability to process, think, and my vision sometimes making things hard to focus on... it's just all crazy. A long list of weird things. I did take a walk on a nice evening and that left me feeling swollen and achy. I want to exercise again, just go for nice walks and not feel tired. So much to come. Our children are back in school and I thought summer would be really long, but no, it's gone! The days are fleeting,

I'm so thankful, ultimately, that God knows me, He knows what I can and can't do, He understands my thoughts and my moods. Moods have been swinging a bit - when you are tired and worn, I find patience with things that you once had them with, are also a bit fleeting :) God has done so much, probably so much more than I even realize through cancer, I have seen others look at me in a different way since having cancer, opportunities to tell my story - His story! Heard this verse yesterday and always reminded of the importance of it –

"Let the words of my mouth and the meditation of my heart be acceptable in thy sight, Oh, Lord, My strength and My redeemer!" (Psalm 19:14 KJV).

May we point others to Christ, May He be our strength and thankful He is my redeemer!

Thank you all again, for all your prayers, words, support! We do not do things alone! We have not walked this journey alone. Alone - I am a person who enjoys being alone, I will enjoy the quiet time provided by God over the next weeks, as the kids are in school. I will rest and spend time with Him... very thankful for the timing of it all. Heidi

3

Remission

With cancer treatments behind us, we began the process of recovery and settling back into life and ministry. Many challenges lay ahead and with cancer now behind us (we thought,) we continued to trust and follow Christ's lead.

August 31, 2013

So, it's Saturday morning and I am still sitting in bed. The week has been so long!!! Longer than most. Long days when you wake up and know you are simply waiting for the days to pass before feeling better. This is the most I have spent in bed... so weak this round, slept 12 hours the other night. After all that sleep you think - Oh, I will feel stronger and then you don't. I am continually thankful that I know this is the last round to fight through, although I find the days a struggle. I have learned to do pretty well at letting things go, but then it just piles up. Mostly, I don't care. Just want to not feel sick. So, almost a week in bed, think I have left the house only 3 times this week... always feels good to get out. Hoping today will start the day of eating normal things again, food is such a struggle...

Well, not much else, we do ask that you continue to pray for me to heal, I think my hair is getting darker, I just prefer to have it :) I won't complain about the color :) I had a dream I woke up and had hair again, crazy dreams were many this week. Please pray for our family too, pray for unity, wisdom, patience. Always, lots going on and we are ready to get back to a new normal.

I will have my repeat CT's in about 3 weeks and then discuss taking out my port. I thought I might just keep it awhile 'til they said I still have to come and get it flushed every 4-6 weeks – no, thank you. Ready for this all to be behind me. Ready to be able to go outside this fall and take a nice walk without feeling exhausted. Doctor says about 6 weeks before I should do too much. I am so thankful for my health, it is truly a blessing, I have always felt that way and now... all the more! God is good and we will continue to trust Him through it all! Heidi

September 12, 2013 – After Chemo...

So, I am over two weeks after my final chemo. As each day comes I have been finding myself frustrated. Not sure what I exactly thought would happen but wasn't this. Most rounds of chemo, I spent several days (5-9) not feeling great, various side effects to deal with. The good part was the days after I felt very close to my normal.

The last two rounds left me with no normal. I have moments I think I feel energy and they are just that, moments. Today I got up for 30 minutes and then went back to bed until 10, got a few things done, thinking I felt okay and just a short time later - feel exhausted. So, I think I'm at about 50 % of what I normally am able to do. I only last an hour or so when it comes to actively running errands - grocery.

As for my ability to think - a real struggle. The calendar is full with activities and each day I need the calendar, to survive, one day at a time. Todd has changed the hours of his work day so he is available to be home to help after school most days or at least to do some picking up, so I'm not running non-stop. My ability to process information is very slow and sometimes just not there. A very frustrating thing.

> We know that God has brought us here and will continue to walk with us through this year... we cannot do any of this on our own!

So, today I got on line just to see how long before my normal may return, and I'm seeing anywhere from 3-6-12 months. Each person is different and so I will just keep resting. Food has been a bit of a struggle. Your appetite and taste buds change so much during chemo that it leaves you... just not really all that hungry. I'm eating, spinach and cheese omelets most days to get things started... trying to find my energy.

As for my hair, it's getting thicker... filling in a bit. Been suggested to take prenatal vitamins because they often help the hair to grow, waiting to see if that's okay from my nurse. One over the counter vitamin said – "if you have a history of cancer consult your Dr." So, we will see what they say.

In October, Todd and I will get a weekend away to go to an adoption conference. We will be adopting our daughter on Oct. 21st! The 10th of October I will have my repeat CT's and meet with the Dr. following for the results. Assumption is that they will be clear as they were a few months ago.

So, one day at a time as always! God is good and teaching us so much. I know that 2013 will be a year that we will not soon forget. We have many more things going on in our life that I cannot share. We know that God has brought us here and will continue to walk with us through this year. He will be faithful to get the glory in the end, we cannot do any of this on our own! Heidi

October 1, 2013

October is upon us! I thought I would give an update although we are mostly on the other side of cancer.

I am finding myself more reflective now that I am through it all... I find myself hearing stories, relating more to others struggles, although I have always thought of myself as one who has done that. I realize that when in the fire, sometimes all you do is get through, it's others, those God places around you that pull you through, they are praying when you are sleeping, weak and worn, they are your strength when you feel like you just can't keep up. I still find that a part of my journey has been alone (meaning me and God) - not completely alone, because God knows all my thoughts and He has dealt with my internal issues.

There are just some things in life you can't explain, you see others try to relate but they can't... each person's journey is just that - theirs to live. We can find strength through others but ultimately we make the internal choices necessary for ourselves to get through the storm. God changes all of us through it, in the way He planned, but each learns and grows in different ways. I find tears a common part of my days lately. I hear, or listen or see something and it just affects me... I am still weak in many ways although my strength is slowly returning.

Health-wise, my big accomplishment this past week has been sleeping through the night on my own! I feel like a Mom with a newborn baby... My sleep had gotten so messed up I had to take medication and I really don't like taking stuff. So, praise God I have had 3 good night's sleep and last night, well, left much to be desired but it's okay. Little signs of life may be coming back to a new normal. I have also gone days without a nap, I think that has helped to sleep all night as well. My appetite, well, really don't have one. I continue to eat but some days it's just whatever is there... I'm just hoping it will all be back to normal in time for Thanksgiving! I love eating what others cook, just deciding what to eat and then making it is a bit of a chore, when nothing sounds good.

> When in the fire, sometimes all you do is get through, it's others, those God places around you that pull you through.

My energy is okay. When you are basically a year behind on household stuff, no amount of energy or time is going to feel sufficient, especially when life and kids and school just keep going... My brain is still missing things, like typing, does some letters backwards when typing but I feel like it's getting better.

So, October is a big month for us! Todd and I will be attending an Adoption Conference. One day for us :) and two days for Conference! Then on the 10th I will have my repeat CT's and see the doctor. Then on the 14th I have an appointment with the general surgeon to schedule my port removal surgery. On the 21st will be Bailey's adoption! Then Fall break which we will need and one other important date at the end of the month on our calendar. So please continue to pray for us! So, a full month, plus dentist appointments, I'm dreading mine, it's been a year, due to timing of diagnosis for me, so hoping I won't need a root canal or crown etc. Seems to always be something.

Life is busy and full and we are so thankful! We got a beautiful picture taken of our family this past weekend and when I look at it, brings tears to my eyes... it's been a long year.

One full of ups and downs but God has been and will always be faithful! I hear the song by Laura Story - what if your blessings come through raindrops, what if healing comes through pain, what if a thousand sleepless nights is what it takes to know you are near... God is near... we could never have gotten through this time in life without Him. He is our strength and salvation, a very present help in times of trouble! Always look around, really take time to SEE those around you and KNOW what is going on in their lives... Be Christ to them, Love them - Heidi

November 5, 2013 – Final Milestone / prayer request (Todd)

Please pray for Heidi today as she has surgery to have her port removed. (Praise that she is in remission / prayer for a quick recovery from the surgery).

November 12, 2013

So, it's 5:07 a.m. and for those of you who know me, I am not a morning person but since I have been laying in bed wide awake since 3:30, thinking, praying and even finding tears streaming from my eyes, I thought maybe it's time to write...

Last week kinda finalized this journey in many ways, my port was removed and I healed rather quickly. I was thankfully only really sore for a few days. I was overwhelmed just now, opening this site to see that over 6,000 times people have looked to read, my story. I feel my story has only begun. Life is so crazy, how we view it, how we look at it all and take it in. How we are able to survive crisis. So, what am I trying to say and share... not sure.

I find that each day now I look in the mirror and I see me, I really look the same as 10 months ago, when I was first diagnosed, minus my hair :) I have no clue what to do with "boy hair" it's growing slowly and not even enough to spike or style quite yet. But anyway, it's hard to look in the mirror and see "normal you" and yet you are not the same, you are changed forever. My body "looks" normal but as my wise husband keeps saying, I am not recovered. My brain wants to just pick up and keep going like I once did. Yesterday I slept 'til 10, that happens at least once a week still... now today, last night, I pay for that by laying in bed tossing and turning, so I'm not sure I'm getting ahead on my sleep, since I didn't sleep. I am struggling with balance in life, expectations, being content. Why is it that God continually brings us full circle, about the time you think you have "gotten" something down, here you find yourself right back learning the same things over again.

How come I keep thinking surviving cancer was easy but this everyday life thing, just might kill me. God has a way of allowing us to survive crisis, but we do just that, survive it, hanging on to all that surrounds us and HIM to pull us through. I could not have done any of it alone. I'm thankful there was a beginning and an end for me and my type of cancer. But I'm realizing in real life, there is no end to struggling and pain... anyone who really knows our family, they know that cancer has just been one part to a year we will not quickly forget. We are and will be changed forever.

There are many thoughts and conversations I have in my head between myself and God on a regular basis, one of which is this - God, I'm in over my head! But - I know in my overwhelmed state that God has me right where He wants me... I've always been a black and white person - I like clear lines, keeps life easy but God has so shaken that up for me this year... I am living my life, not someone else's, I cannot look at others and say what they should or shouldn't do, I have not walked their path. God alone walks in my shoes with me 24 hours a day, others only get a glimpse of the struggle. I, myself, deny much of the struggle along the way, part of the surviving a crisis - but it catches up with us and then we have to stop and deal. So, I guess that's where I am - stopping and dealing... I want to be mad at myself, saying - Heidi, just be thankful! you are alive and well... well, again, I may be saying something I shouldn't and maybe

I will be told by someone who loves me to delete this but - dying or choosing to give up is the easy part of life, living is the hard part, trusting, choosing, dealing.

God is at work... and when life doesn't make sense and I don't know what He is doing,... I will still choose to trust Him!

So, don't fret, my life is grounded in my faith! God is good, He is faithful... I believe and my hope is in Him... but let's be real, it's hard! So, I am picking up the pieces to a really hard year, a year that will change me and my family and those around me forever. I don't like change... :) but I am beginning to see some really great things God has been doing while I have been struggling. I know that His picture, the end picture, is one I can trust Him with. It will be beautiful... there are days I long for heaven, I'm ready, Lord! Physical and emotional exhaustion are here... I have minor health issues I'm still dealing with but most importantly God is at work... and when life doesn't make sense and I don't know what He is doing,... I will still choose to trust Him! There is so much more and some days I think maybe I need to start a blog, I have no time to read others and I hate the computer, since it does not like me but who knows... life is not meant to be done alone and I'm thankful that I have had amazing people loving and praying for me and my family. Thank You! Please continue to pray... I know we need Christ first in our lives and then we need each other. We need to not have views and opinions about where others are in life, we need to just come along side them, pray and love on them. For now, that's all I have - Love you all! Heidi

*As life began to get back to normal,
Heidi went for a few months without posting*

March 6, 2014

So, once again, I am awake far too early for me. I laid in bed last night thinking it might be time to post an update and so here I am.

It's funny how we have expectations of how life will go and then, at least for me, it never goes that way. I really was excited about 2014 and how I was going to have some time to rest and recover from all of last year but God has had other plans. 2014 has come in with a giant bang and the snow continually has added to it. Rest? well, at some level I am getting it, but not the way I had hoped. God does things His way, I am STILL learning that. I think that is why I have an issue with planning things. If I plan anything, even one day, it never goes as planned. Just too many people and things to balance, something always changes.

On February 14, I had my Oncologist appointment. It was Valentine's Day so I baked all week and took tons of cookies to my Dr., Nurse and the Chemo wing at the hospital. My sweet 8-year-old made a heart that thanked them for taking care of her Mommy, while she had cancer and making her better. My Nurse spent a chunk of time visiting with us. She was amazing through the whole process. She tells us, we are a Special couple, as she listens to our life and all God has done in the last year. He has used us to minister to her. Our Dr. spent at least 45 minutes with us, talking, visiting and showing us all my past scans, the ones with cancer and then the ones without. Pretty neat to see. Then we discussed treatment for this year. He agreed that it's just protocol to run scans and bloodwork over and over to make sure, so we discussed a bit more relaxed plan for this year. 3 month check-ups and then Chest CT's twice this year. The assumption is nothing will be found but this will keep a close eye on my health and present any red flags if there are any to be found. We will pray that cancer is a part of my past but have to admit as he speaks, I had moments of what if's. Reality is, if cancer comes back, we do what we did last year. Not fun but God pulled us through and we are confident He will do it again. In many ways, cancer for me was just a time of getting through it, I saw an end and always believed it would come. Nowadays, everyday life seems to be more challenging than cancer was... I know that probably makes no sense. Every day we are presented with challenges, struggles, pain, those we love hurting. It has already been a great year of loss... seems people all around us are dying. School friends for my children and also for myself, extended family members, all unexpected loss, such young life. Life is hard to understand at times.

I am just reminded that God uses all things and all people to impact others around them. So, the question is, what kind of impact am I having, or are you having? Every day we get up and often do the same things over and over, but Know that God has you where He wants you. You are touching the lives of those around you and they, You! Do they see Christ in you? Not perfection, but a real person. One who loves, one who forgives, one who cares, one who has time to listen and invest in them... or

Life is full of questions we don't get answers to, life is full of waiting when we don't understand. Bottom line, God is God! He is good, He can be trusted, even through the pain...

are we just about ourselves, our lives, our families. Oh, those are important things but giving of ourselves to others changes us and them forever. I think of Jesus, one quality He has that I don't do well at is, I believe He was gentle. He was never rushed, harsh, impatient, I just don't see it in the scriptures. He was angry at sin, but patient and loving with the sinner, He had time for others... His life was never about himself... remember He gave up His life for us! True love, true sacrifice... ask yourself what are love and sacrifice? you will find the answer much deeper than you anticipated. I am reminded how selfish I am, and everyone else too :) sorry, truth is truth.

I am also reminded of this, life is full of questions we don't get answers to, life is full of waiting when we don't understand. Bottom line, God is God! He is good, He can be trusted, even through the pain... His ultimate goal is to make us more like Him. Are you becoming more like Him? Is He changing you? Are you letting Him? Just last night I laid in bed with a smile on my face. After praying for over 10 years about a situation, God brought an answer! 10 years, seems life forever but I was reminded of God's timing, God's way... His ways are perfect and His ways are not our ways...

I will end with something more light hearted – Hair :) So, I don't really have any pictures because I don't have a smart phone and I don't take selfies:) but it's coming in well... it's brown and not blonde anymore, it is also curly! Craziness... but honestly, I like it. I just wet it down, put mousse on it and it's done. No real options for styling yet but the curl is making it easier, I'm actually thankful for the curl, better than just straight short hair I can't do anything with. I see this as God being kind to me, After having no hair, it's at least nice to not have to stress about how bad my hair looks, now that I do have it :) It's still very cold! but short will be nice for summer.

Overall, I feel healthy. The weather is dragging me down and I'm so ready to hear the birds sing, sit outside and watch the kids play. Go for a walk, not on snow and ice :) I do believe God has healed me and with Spring will also come more energy. Being in the house is tiring to everyone. I do have one request. Since August, my right hand swells badly every night, also causes pain in my fingers at times. This week, I had a few days where it hurt most of the day as well. This is very frustrating and the aching and pain gets old at times. If, I've learned one thing though - it's that you can adjust to anything over time. However, some answers would be lovely. My Dr. seems to think it unrelated to Chemo, I seem to disagree. My hope it that in time it will just go away! Yes, without having to see more Dr. who seem to have no answers. They don't seem to be concerned and so most of the time I too, am not concerned but then there are those days you brain says - what if it is something? God knows best and will care for me, discussed with my Dr. that my original blood work would have never caused any red flags for any Dr. It did not indicate elevated counts that would have caused any Dr. to think I had cancer. Thankful for the swollen lymph node that indicated cancer. God does and has taken care of me and I am so thankful.

So, as always I have a lot to say :) but now I will start my day, knowing a nap will be in my future :) Have a great day and know that even when your day is not great! God is! Heidi

June 30, 2014 – Tomorrow

Today I add a journal update... tomorrow I will see a new ENT Dr. at the University of Chicago. Just a few short weeks ago I called my Oncology Nurse and said a word I didn't want to ever have to say again, biopsy. I need a biopsy. I had discussed with my Oncologist just a month earlier that I had found a swollen lymph node in my neck. Over 3 weeks it grew and had not gone away. He knows me well and was content to allow me to give it a few more weeks. He said, maybe inflammation from sickness, but as always I have not been sick. He said it is not characteristic of Lymphoma because it was really sore and continues to give me discomfort each day, not all day just when I yawn or move my head at night on my pillow.

So, it's time to know again what is going on with my body. Over all I feel well. I am always tired but we live a pretty busy and stressful life so I'm not sure that is an indicator of a problem. Tomorrow I will only see the Dr. so he can decide what and where he wants to biopsy and then he will schedule. Please pray the procedure is easy and more importantly that the results give us answers. I don't want to hear cancer again but I also don't want to be negligent, I have much to live for! God never ceases to place opportunities to minister into my life and I'm simply not done doing all He has for me to do. He is faithful and just praying for good results.

My PET in Oct was clear and I never had cancer in my neck, it was all in my chest, so logic says, it's something else, please pray with us.

Thank you in advance and I will keep you updated as I know more. We do have a praise, we just received notice from the hospital that they will cover 75% of our bills this year! God is good, have a great day! Heidi

July 3, 2014

July has arrived and the weather is crazy and cool. Actually thankful since we got hit pretty hard from the storm going 36 hours without electricity, had to clean up 30 ft. of tree in the back yard, no air in the house, and more than 2 days without internet. It's amazing our children have survived. I was actually asked "what did people do before electronics? "One resorted to reading, imagine that and lots of nice family time... I have enjoyed the down time from media.

Well, as for the beginning of Tuesday before the storm... did you know that Psalm 112: 7 says *"They will have no fear of bad news; their hearts are steadfast, trusting in the LORD."* I found that verse sometime before when I was sick, I was amazed at the clear words of scripture.

So, bottom line is this, on July 8th I will have a neck CT. I am thankful I did not have this done in April because so much has changed in my neck since April and they would have just made me do it again, and charged me again. Little blessings, is what I see. So then, on Thursday he had an appointment open up and I took it, I will have surgery. The CT will determine if he takes the whole node, or if there is danger due to the location and if he will think just take a few pieces and send them to pathology. At this point we know nothing, don't even know what to think. He said they will run a full pathology due to my history and if it's not cancer they will then work to find out what it IS. He said, I'm sure you would like that lump out of your neck... yes, yes, I would. My Oncology nurse was right, we really liked this Dr, so I am thankful for that. I feel they will be thorough and take good care of me. I'll just say that just being in the Dr. office and talking about it all causes stress and wonder... but I am confident that nothing happens outside of God and His plan and we will just wait. Waiting and trusting seem to often be the theme of my life. This weekend we will enjoy time celebrating and having fun with family, not worrying.

> I am confident that nothing happens outside of God and His plan and we will just wait. Waiting and trusting seem to often be the theme of my life.

So, after the physical storm passed late on Tuesday night and I got up early and walked on Wednesday morning, I thought how we are like the trees. The one in our back yard, its roots strong but it lost a huge portion that was weak and taken out in the storm. Sometimes we are that tree, our roots are strong but the storm leaves damage, leaves weakness but we must keep standing strong and growing those roots deep, we are not taken out.

When I walked out our front door the neighbor's tree (100 ft. tall, minimally) was completely up rooted. I sit and look at that tree all the time, it looks fine, looks strong but the roots, dead! I realized, that is many in life. They look like they are great and strong but their roots, in the ground, or deep in their hearts, it's unhealthy, weak, or even dead. No one knew the tree was that way, now we do. The storm took it out.

This storm caused much thinking about life, roots, etc. Kate's devotion yesterday was titled, Two Trees :) God always brings things full circle. I shared my thoughts with her and at some level I think her 9-year-old brain connected, seeing the visual right in front of her eyes. Also, thankful for neighbors who are amazing. They all pitched together and helped one another in different ways. God is always giving opportunities for our lives to interact with others, do we take them? How deep are your roots grounded in the only Truth! God and His Word! Will the next storm - take you out? or will it only change you forever all the while your roots are deep in the Truth! Life is always changing, although we always want to believe we have control, God ultimately is the controller of all. Life changes in a moment, be thankful, love others, live outside of yourself, dig deep into God and His Word, be changed forever in a good way, don't be the dead tree.

Thank you all for praying. It helps me to know and be reminded that life is not done alone! God gives us what we need, He gives us support, strength and prayer reminds us we are dependent on Him! and Him alone. This life is not about us, it's about Him, sharing Him with others! May He be glorified through us! Have a Great 4th of July weekend! Heidi

July 9, 2014 – Biopsy

Tomorrow I will have my biopsy at 11:45 at the University of Chicago. Yesterday I took the train into town and had my CT done on my neck. This CT will allow the Dr. to have a clear picture of what he will do during tomorrow's surgery, so we will find out when we get there. I was thankful for no rain on my trip yesterday, the weather was really great for walking from the train. I was just thankful as always that I made the train on time, got on the right train and somehow made it there and back with no issues :) Since I hit construction on the way and thought I had missed my train on the way back, just glad to be home. I am thankful for my faithful driver (love you, Todd) I choose not to drive into the city, too much stress for me to do alone and too many trips lately.

My CT appointment was at 2:30 and due to the "need to arrive 30 minutes early" I was Done at 2:35 because they were on time, fast and always really awesome in that radiology department.

So, today I wake up feeling super tired (wearing flip flops yesterday was not a good idea, never again, feeling it physically) plan to just take it easy today. I don't do "taking it easy" very well. So, please pray that I will feel rested going into surgery tomorrow. I think my biggest concern for tomorrow, other than diagnosis, is how uncomfortable an incision in the middle of my neck will be. I like my sleep and get frustrated when pain and discomfort rob me of it. So, please pray for little discomfort and pain. Also, I had a complication after this same surgery last time that landed me in the ER first thing the next morning. Praying for no complications. And one other small thing, that the nurse I have will understand why I do NOT want an IV in my hand for surgery, leaving me with blown up veins. I plan to let them know we need another option. Usually they let the resident "try first" too, not cool. Lots of fun, little things when it comes to surgery. Wish I didn't know them all :) Tomorrow will come and go and I imagine it will be a week before we will know anything. Will post as soon as we know anything. Thanks for all your prayers! They are greatly appreciated... Heidi

July 11, 2014 – After surgery

Good Morning friends and family. If you are on FB I think Todd put a small update you may have seen. I do really well going into surgery but always forget how much I hate the after.

I did not ever see or talk with the Dr. Apparently I was a bit out of it but Todd said that he only removed half of the node. The rest was attached to the muscle and artery. The cut looks like he removed the whole thing, not a pretty site. I knew it would be more sore on my neck, we use the neck muscles to swallow, yawn, sneeze, move really :) more than we realize. After much moving around last night I'm thankful I found a comfortable position and got plenty of sleep. I feel okay today, rest wise. I feel super sore and pain medication only knocks me out, doesn't care for the pain. I think I need to ask for a different kind. So, I will take it very easy today, resting and maybe reading. Promised Kate a movie in bed together :)

I appreciate all your prayers... sometimes you just have to get through stuff. My nurse was wonderful and honored my "no IV in the hand" request. She took care of me. I was out cold leaving for surgery and I remember nothing. I have had no after surgery complications, as I did last time and I only got a bit irritated after surgery, with my post op nurse but I think we worked things out :) My throat is a bit irritated, not sure if they put a tube down it for surgery but kinda feels that way... Todd is off to get my favorite popsicles!... and I'm just real achy.

Please pray it only last a few days. I am really not a person who stresses about more than just today, one day at a time BUT I must say after the reminder of being in the hospital, the sites, smells, the nausea that comes after surgery, meds and pain... I am really praying and having some talks with God about good results. Todd says it will probably be 5 plus days before we have results. My mind is a bit stressed wondering about how I would repeat last year's surgeries and chemotherapy, not good memories. So, as I know you are, please pray with us. My oncologist will call with the results and he is awesome and will call as soon as he has them, I'm sure.

For now, I rest and we all wait... God seems to think I need to wait a lot... never fun but keeps us dependent

July 17, 2014 – Test results

So, I am still reeling from the phone call, the results are cancer again. My Dr. says the area is small but it's still Lymphoma and must be treated. I responded well to the chemotherapy before but unfortunately with the return of the Lymphoma we will have to do chemo again and he says a different regiment. After chemo he says it will be followed up with stem cell replacement therapy. I honestly don't know what all that means at this time and really don't care to know. I did a bit of research and did not like what I read, my version, this next journey will be worse than the first.

I have always been a one day at a time person and that skill in life will continue to be the one that keeps me grounded... So, not much to say or even think. I know my foundation, which is God is always in control and has not lost control, but reality is, I still have feelings and thoughts... I have shared them with God and I will not share them with y'all :) some things must be between He and I as we walk this journey together with the support of all those who love us.

As for today, all our kids are gone for the week, again timing is good - giving me time to process and mentally deal with reality. They do not know yet. I feel good. I struggle with the reality that in order to not have cancer they have to make me sick, even though I don't feel sick, in order to make me better. I think first time through you don't know what to expect and sometimes doing things over is a bit worse, simply because you do know what to expect. So, I have told my Dr. I need a little time. I will start with scans in the next couple weeks and then when I decide I am ready I will have my port put back in... dreading that. I am thankful to have had it removed... I really didn't like it but now I'm sure it will be my hated friend for a long while. School starts on the 20th of August and I really don't want to have surgery and then start chemo 'til after that but I feel a bit of resistance on my Doctor's

> God is good, don't doubt that, it's the foundation of faith that keeps us going when fear seeks to weaken us!

end... I want to enjoy the last 6 weeks of summer with my children and hubby, not too much to ask before sickness takes over. Life has not seemed to have given me a break and that's one of the conversations God and I have had :) but I know God will see us through, I think no matter what, when life is hard we always have this thought come to mind, why me, God? Why this? I was confident this was a journey of the past, that is what helped me get through it the first time but now to do it over again... struggles.

So, for not knowing what to say, I think for now, I have said plenty... Thank you in advance for your prayers and support and I know over the next months we will become even better friends as we share our lives together, again! Heidi

July 22, 2014 – Small update

So, I will be going in for my scans and to see the Dr. on July 31st. I am actually happy about this, I didn't want to make two trips and the fact that they couldn't get me in this week, is okay with me. I am using the time to get organized for the journey and to spend time with my family and friends. Each day, right now is a good day. I feel good and for that I'm thankful. God says, "Do not worry about tomorrow" so I'm not worrying, I am however preparing :)

I have said before I hate waiting... I smiled to myself yesterday and said, "Lord, I am fine with waiting now" Perspective change. I am however thankful to know some of what is to come. Helps to mentally prepare and remind myself, although this will be different, I have done it before and we will come through it again. We had amazing prayer warriors and support and we will have that again.

I honestly have non-stop thoughts about much lately. In time, those things will come to completion in my mind and I will share but for today I am off to enjoy the sunshine and get some things done, while I can do :) For, those who don't know, I am a doer, not to be confused with a planner, or someone who is organized, I am far from that. I love people and friends and getting stuff done. I learned last time while sick, I really was able to sit on the couch with the house messy or dishes undone and not care... it truly is possible :) Those things ultimately, don't matter. Just rambling now, thank you all for your continued support. Just pray for great moments and memories in these final weeks before sickness takes over for a time. Not looking forward to my brain disappearing again... but at least I know it returns :) God is good, don't doubt that, it's the foundation of faith that keeps us going when fear seeks to weaken us! Have an amazing day! Heidi

July 23, 2014 (Todd)

The weekend after we heard the news, I posted a blog article entitled "How to (and how NOT to) Minister to Families Battling Cancer."[10] In the article I shared those things from my own experience that I found helpful and not so helpful as people responded to our news. The article linked to by Tim Challies and others and has, in just a few days, been viewed thousands of times and shared on social media over 800 times. I am thankful that my thoughts could be so helpful to others. I pray that many people will be helped to minister to others in their time of need. I am thankful for our own support system both online and here at home. We have so many supportive friends and family, and a wonderful church family. Thank you all!

July 31, 2014 – What the journey will look like

So, I am still processing and choosing some denial for now. My day ran smooth, the scan guy is awesome and always makes it a positive experience and they are thorough and on time. Thankful.

Thought I was ready to hear just about anything but no, the Dr. surprised me with it all. Honestly, I will not have all the details in this update or most of them even right, probably :) Basically, I will have a completely different regiment. I will be hospitalized for 3-4 days for each treatment, it's called ICE (not sure what that stands for but I'm sure some of you Dr/Nurse sorts will know). There will be two of those treatments and then scans. If the scans are good they will do one more, so 3 treatments total, over 9 weeks. However, unlike my last chemo rounds if my counts are too low they will wait and not proceed until my counts are good. He also threw in there something about a daily shot of some sorts, wishing I knew a nurse on my block! Guess, Todd will have to do, I'm not sticking a needle in myself... After these rounds then I will get a few weeks off. Then I will be hospitalized for 2-3 weeks for some intense high chemo over several days and then I think when my counts are good they will do the stem cell therapy. Whew!!!! I know there is also additional blood draws, a major draw of my cells and high risk of infections and lots of another not really cool stuff. I think sometimes it's best to just get some of the details.

Any of you who know me well, know I am a one day at a time person. I simply cannot worry about tomorrow or I would be a mess. I will enjoy today and tomorrow will just do one day at a time. However, there is much planning to do. Tomorrow I will schedule my Port surgery, probably for the 11th of August is my plan and looks like my first treatment will be August 28th. I will talk with my nurse tomorrow and then I will get more things nailed down. For now, just needing time to process and get some things in order for the next phase of life. We will need much prayers and support and much more love and support for my hubby and kids. Funny, how when you are the sick one you are the one worrying about everyone else. It's a lot - let's be honest. God is in control and I simply do not know why this journey again and more intense this time, but I'm confident He never loses control and will walk with us through this, making us stronger through the process. I will thank you in advance for everything and the many prayers. I know we did not do this alone before and will not do it alone again. I think this time, it's a little scarier for us all but again, we continue to trust... Thank you all! Heidi

August 2, 2014 – Still processing and re-typing since it just got deleted :)

So, starting over... I have been doing Beth Moore's study - Living Beyond Yourself. This week is about Sacrificial Submission - I see it as my attitude towards suffering that God is placing in my life and those that I love. It's speaking of gentleness and a bunch of Greek stuff... I am not a scholar of any sorts but it says – "an inward grace of the soul, calmness toward God in particular."[11] The acceptance of God's dealings with us considering them as good in that they enhance the closeness of our relationship. Oh, I want an inner calmness, I want a close relationship with Christ but I don't think any of us would be quick to say that we will be happy to have those things through suffering.

No one likes suffering or the idea that it is coming and you can do nothing about it. I struggle today with Philippians 3:10. How was Paul so confident so able to say *"I want to know Christ and the power of his resurrection* (I'm good with this part, you too?) *and the fellowship of his suffering..."* "I think I would like to stop there. I do agree with the saying "to endure pain and suffering in the will of God, is far better than to risk ease outside of His faithful hands"[12] but in our humanness I think there is always a But... at least for where I am now... know I'm in God's will, I know He will care for me, for us. I am eternally grateful for my foundations in Christ and all that I know and have learned and believe, it is truly what keeps me going.

In 2 Corinthians 6 is a list of Paul's sufferings, sickness, pain, no sleep, hunger... I see much of this on its way. Then these deep phrases for meditating on... sorrowful, yet always rejoicing... dying, yet we live on... poor, yet making many rich... having nothing yet possessing everything... Wow.

I have always been a person who felt, I needed God. I never felt like I could just go out and get the most amazing job, or do years of schooling and be at the top of my class, I'm just not that kind of person. I'm just simple. I just like people (most of the time :) and building relationships, helping, serving, doing... but I've always felt I needed Christ to accomplish those things. I feel many of us go through every day and we would say "sure, I need Christ" but do you really need Him??? Are you really depending on Him today, seeking Him? thankful to Him because every breath, every dollar, everything that you have and possess belongs to Him... do you take time to realize this. I have to admit... I haven't always but... I don't think any of us will ever achieve the ability to always keep life in perspective but today ask yourself where are you? is there a closeness in your relationship with God or are you the one "getting stuff done" and God is just in the back ground. I am in a place where I don't need Him, every hour... but every minute of every day, clinging tight, knowing He will sustain me. I don't plan on going anywhere and I hope God and I are on the same page in that regard... none of us are guaranteed tomorrow or even our next breath... So thank you for taking this journey with me. I will be writing on here as my brain fills up and I need to process, unless Todd sets up a different avenue for sharing but I feel this one is good.

In the spirit of the word gentleness... Beth writes from a story... Her tears were not those of resistance. They were tears of submission: knowing that the end was worth the means."[13] It is hard to have that attitude but with Christ we know He does nothing without a purpose... I feel Paul thought it an honor to suffer for Christ, I am still working on being okay with suffering, hate hospitals and certain smells and pain and the list goes on but Christ goes before me and an army will be praying and my hubby will be close by my side... helping me and loving me when I get a little crazy with the Dr. and nurses... it's only happened a few times. Again, not big on pain and suffering and confident I will NOT get used to it:) but I will press on and be thankful that 4 months is just another small journey, not a lifetime... thanks for listening... My port surgery will be on August 11th at 9 a.m. I am thankful that they have agreed to make sure this a better experience than the last time (long story and not a good one) but the lady on the phone was very kind and promises me I will be comfortable and cared for... each Dr. and Nurse you encounter helps to ease the way... so continually praying for the best ones :) Enjoy today! Heidi

4

Round Two

Our second round of cancer and treatments was more serious than the first. A more intensive regimen and less favourable prognosis drove us to a deeper level of dependence on God. Still, He remained faithful!

August 10, 2014 – Port

So, surgery is at 9 a.m. on Monday morning. We will drop Max off at Football practice and head to the hospital... then we will pick him up after :) Life doesn't seem to stop. I am very thankful I have talked to two great nurses in regards to this surgery... I had some issues with this surgery last time. They promise to take good care of me...

As for Chemo starting that should be on the 28th. When I called to schedule they told me they don't schedule it, they just call me that day and let me know if a bed is available... What?? I thought finding out the day before surgeries what time surgery would be was inconvenient, this is crazy. Although, I get it and understand why it's the case the scheduling stuff is very stressful with all we have to balance. So please pray for things to just fall into place. Thankful for flexible friends and family who we are lining up to help with all the many things. God has taken care of us and I know He will continue to.

I think we have all begun to deal with the reality of the next 4 months. One breakdown at a time. I said this week "it's just too much" and Todd said, "yes, it is." Life is hard at times and so overwhelming... I love the verse, when my heart is overwhelmed - lead me to the ROCK that is higher than I. We are His children and He loves us and will care for us. Thankful for the armies of prayer warriors on our behalf and I'm content to place myself in the care of the Dr. and Nurses that God will give me over the next several months. Pray for strength for me and for Todd as he runs a marathon trying to do all I usually do. I am hopeful that after the first round I will have a better idea what the rest of the journey will be like. Pray for our kids as life will change much more this round. I have seen that this time, the process is causing fear, none of us likes to face fear. Fear tries to crush our Faith but anyone who has great Faith knows that Faith will win out over Fear, we must keep our eyes on Christ... He always wins, we always win! He will care for us... Heidi

August 11, 2014 – After Port

So, thankful today went smooth. They did take good care of me at the hospital today and a little extra meds to get me through. I felt really good

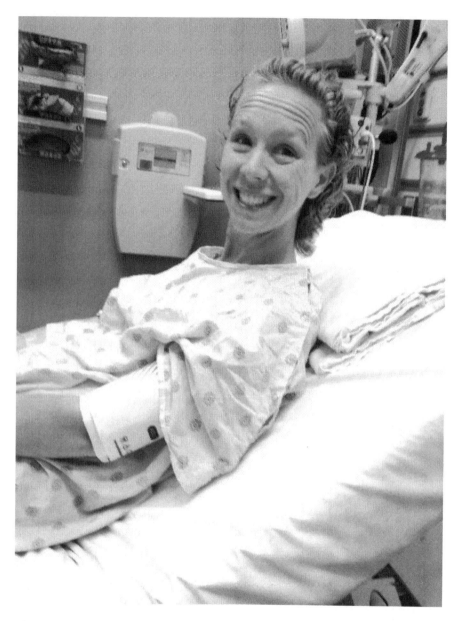

when I woke up. The nurse gave me some juice and Oreo's and said I was ready to go home. I felt ready, like I hadn't even had surgery. I am laughing now realizing they just sent me out of recovery told me to go down the hall, take the elevator and my husband would meet me there with the car. I'm laughing because I remember all this but I really don't. I can't believe they just sent me on my own... I remember being asleep the lobby and getting into the car with Todd, thankfully it was him :) I think anyone probably could have taken me and I would have just slept. Apparently unless you get a general anesthesia that's the only way the wheel you down and last time too, they still just left me there for Todd to come find me. Funny, how they do things.

Todd got me some food and I really do remember eating it but only kinda... came home crawled into bed feeling okay, just sleepy. But when I woke up and all the medication had worn off, well OUCH is a good word. Like I've been shot twice, so basically don't move your neck, right arm or cough, Oh, really don't cough. I think something might rupture. So, just looking back through what I posted after my last Port and apparently I described it as a hole in my chest kinda feeling, yep! That's it! and apparently they told me last time to take Tylenol too, and I took Vicodin... Tylenol doesn't always take care of a headache but they think it's going to fix this, too funny!

So, I have the whole week to rest, pain is always worse the first several days. I do feel very rested so I'm in a better mindset to handle the pain. We got a movie to watch as a family tonight so I will see if I can make it through... Thank you again for all your prayers, one more thing done on the check list and I was laughing again that they say, Oh, we can access your port as soon as we place it in... not on me!!! I'm going to heal before you start any more things on me, but thanks! One pain at a time... Have a great week! Heidi

August 23, 2014 – Overwhelmed...

I have planned often to post an update and words are just too many. Today, I will try... I have been overwhelmed so much in the last few weeks. Much to do, that is overwhelming. Emotions, they come at unexpected time. Thinking of going in the hospital brings butterflies to my stomach and I don't feel like eating. Overwhelmed by the goodness of God and His timing...

Fear is another feeling that tries to overwhelm. I have found it interesting that I was reading about Fear. Don't let you fear be greater than your faith... then I went to an appt. and she had it on her board for the day... then I got a note from my sister yesterday and it had the same phrase... Fear seeks to try and control us. The devil tries to use fear to weaken our faith, Where Great Faith lives destructive fear cannot...

Then I have this song and verse from Psalm 90:12 "Teach me to number my days" I keep thinking only 5 days until I go in the hospital, only... I am numbering my days in a sense. David was trying to get us to see that they are numbered we just get so busy with life who thinks about death, but those who might have a reason to. Honestly, first diagnosis they told me, you have "the best" kind of cancer to have, it will likely never return, it's treatable. I just said okay and what's next. I never thought I would die. Reality is I don't think I will now, because who wants to think that way. I think this is serious and sure I could but one day at a time. I think if we all stop and think, reality is yes, I have cancer and maybe you don't, but either of us could die today or tomorrow. It's not about cancer. We must stop and embrace today, this moment before it's gone... we are not promised tomorrow, no matter who we are. Each day a blessing... but how quickly we forget, even myself. Make sure you know where you are going when you die... if not ask me :)

There seem to be many Christian songs about waves, and oceans and God being in the storm with us. I just heard a new one... "You make me Brave,"[14] I like that saying... it truly is God who gives us the strength and helps us be brave when life is scary and unpredictable. I keep telling my kids, press into God, know Him, talk to Him, you need Him more than you realize. I can't do life without that intimacy. Prayer is about depending on Him accepting - He can, I cannot! This song also says... "Your love in wave after wave, crashes over me... because You are for us, You are not against us... Champion of Heaven you made a way for all to enter." If you don't know God, seek Him! He promises, if you seek him with your whole heart you will find Him. I need Him, not sure about you!

If you don't know God, seek Him! He promises, if you seek him with your whole heart you will find Him.

I am reading a little book about Psalm 23, *"He makes us to lie down in green pastures"*... It says one of the "marks of a Christian should be a serene sense of gentle contentment."[15] I laughed when I read this, should I not be honest? :) I think I'm missing the mark... serene :) gentle and contentment all together... The Bible says, 1 Tim 6:6 *"Godliness with contentment is great gain."* Oh, I believe these things but how is it possible to achieve them in this life... Yes, you are right, not alone, only through Christ. Paul says he *"learned to be content"* (Phil 4:11) and I say... learning to be content and learning to trust God are things we will learn over and over in this life... and some day will be perfected in heaven in me and not until then. Life is hard, but I'm learning...

So, today I was overwhelmed by God's goodness and timing. Our truck died last night, still waiting to be diagnosed... possibly the transmission in which case we will get nothing out of the truck and we are not in a great place for buying a car... but we really need another one... so at 11 p.m. our daughter called to say, the truck was not starting... at 10 a.m. my sister called to ask if we wanted their truck because they were going to look today for a new one... I cried... overwhelmed... We are confident that God will bring us through this next season, and He will provide for us... He has been faithful.

I am continuing to not focus on Thursday but thoughts are beginning to creep in as it gets closer. Like, how awful am I really going to feel... I have read little and know little, for me, that is best... this time. Not an option whether or not to go through the treatment... so I will do my best to not stress about what is coming. I love you all and we are so thankful for your love and support of us and our whole family. We have seen many details come together over the last few weeks and we are reminded, like today, that God has this!!!! even when I doubt and even when I fear... He has this! Last week we had a family gathering, an end of the year cook out at our house (about 50 people) some traveling, lots of shopping- we are ready for a "long winter" stocked! I had some days I felt completely exhausted but doing my best to enjoy every moment and rest.

I know this was long... I will end with some requests... Pray I will get into the hospital on Thursday, I assume it will be evening. Pray for Great nurses... pray for peace and anxiety to be minimal. Funny, I would get sick every time I went to the hospital after a few round of chemo... I was always confused... I really was not mentally stressed, my nurse said, my mind and body just knew... such a strange thing... Pray for physical comfort and that I will maintain a healthy weight... food has been a struggle for me already and chemo does not help. Pray for minimal side effects. Pray for our kids... they will not be with us for 4 days and I know they will be prone to worry... it will be really hard. Pray they will be busy and distracted! Pray for Todd who will be right by my side... so thankful for that, advocating for me... and doing a very hard thing, simply watching...

I keep asking is it harder to be the sick one or to watch someone you love be sick?... I think they might be equals... I will say, my port healing has been great and the port in general does not bother me. Last time it had a life of its own, would bother my sleep and ache etc. but not this time. I occasionally feel like I have a heavy necklace shifted to the right side of my neck, when I go to adjust I realize, Oh, it's my port... thankful it's better this time. Little blessings. Oh, one last thing. I had a lot of right hand swelling since after chemo... no one can figure out why. Only when I lay down... I will be doing a lot of laying in the hospital next week... it has gotten a bit worse since I had my port placed but last night it was really good. Pray for good nights and much rest... I know that's a lot, thanks! Heidi

August 24, 2014 –The storm before the storm (Todd)

I've described this week as the "storm before the storm." For me, it has been like those homeowners on the coast getting ready for the hurricane that is about to make landfall. There are so many things to do to get ready before the storm hits. I usually get two questions – How is Heidi doing? And How am I doing? As far as Heidi, you can see from her posts that she has a deep and consistent faith in the Lord. Yes, there are anxieties and emotions, but the overriding thing I see in her is a trust in the faithfulness of God no matter the circumstance. God has continued to show himself faithful in our lives and has been with us through every storm, we know that he will be with us now.

As for how I am doing, several adjectives come to mind: overwhelmed, tired, helpless, afraid, alone – I've experienced all those emotions and more over the past two weeks. I'm also juggling a number of concerns – concerned about our schedule, my children, our church, the logistics of multiple hospital stays, and our personal finances. Most of the time, though, I will tell you that I'm doing OK. And I'm finding that God can handle my emotions and my concerns. I too know that He is faithful.

I really don't know what God will do. But I DO know His character. I know his promises. I know his record. And I trust Him.

I've done a lot of thinking – too much really – about the serious nature of what is happening here. When you fall into the 5% whose Hodgkin's is NOT cured by the first round of chemo, the cancer becomes a much bigger deal! The prognosis and treatment are quite serious. And, our other challenges don't go away just because Heidi has cancer. It comes down to me that my faith does not depend on how God answers my prayers or handles my circumstances. I believe that everything will work out – I HAVE to – but what if it doesn't? I believe that we will get through this –but what if we don't? I know that God will heal Heidi – but what if He doesn't? What if everything falls apart? What if the worst happens? My mind goes through a million scenarios that begin with "What if... "And an even bigger question: Will I still believe God is faithful even if...?!?

And it comes down to this. My faith is not rooted in a God who will cause everything to turn out just the way I want (need). I desperately need God to come through for me here – I need Heidi to be healed. But my faith is not rooted in whether or not he heals her. I believe that God WILL heal Heidi, but her healing is not a condition of my faith. Rather, my faith is rooted in the character of God – who He is. He is good. He is faithful. He loves me. He is FOR me. He's already given me and Heidi eternal life and forgiveness – His grace – and that grace is sufficient. I'm believing God for healing in Heidi's life, I need Him to heal her. But I'm facing the reality as we start this journey again that I really don't know what God will do. But I DO know His character. I know his promises. I know his record. And I trust Him. God does not always do what we ask him to do. But He is always faithful!

August 26, 2014 – People keep asking how they can help... (Todd)

Only a couple days before chemo begins and we've been getting ready. It's been amazing all the little ways God provides. With all the logistics of hospital stays, me being Mr. Mom and chief care-taker, and expenses piling up, we are seeing God continue to provide. People are lining up to help us with driving, keeping the kids, and helping me with caring for Heidi. Several pastors are on standby to fill in at church when I am with Heidi in the hospital. Our church gave us a needed raise and has been understanding about my need to be with Heidi during her weekend chemo treatments. Heidi already mentioned the gift we received when our truck died. It's wonderful, in a time of need, to see the outpouring of love and concern for our family! We praise the Lord for using so many people to care for us!

People continue to ask us what they can do to help and so I wanted to share three tangible and practical ways you can help us:

1. Assistance with our financial need. Quite honestly, one of our biggest needs remains a financial one. Even with decent insurance and the hospital writing off part of the bill, cancer is expensive. Co-pays for every visit, travel, food while in the hospital, add to the cost over and above our high deductible and out of pocket max. On the one hand, it's only money and I'll gladly pay/borrow any amount of money to beat this cancer – I'll worry about the cost later. On the other hand, as new bills arrive to add to the existing debt from our previous battle, it causes a fair amount of stress.

If you're looking for a way to help us, a gift in any amount would be greatly appreciated. Please don't feel like you have to give– there are a lot of fundraisers out there you can give to and we already know you love and care about us. Also, we trust God with our finances as we do with Heidi's cancer. At the same time, as people have asked what they can do to help, this is one practical and tangible way.

2. Send letters, cards, and encouraging notes. Over the next few months, Heidi will be spending extended time away from people for hospital stays and recovery time. I've found that she is always encouraged when she receives personal notes and cards from people in the mail. Between now and thanksgiving, would you write and/or send cards to Heidi? I know she will be encouraged.

3. Prayer. Our biggest request and need is for your prayers. Would you add Heidi and I and our kids to your prayer list and lift us up before the Father regularly. Pray for the family to continue to trust the Lord through each step of the journey. Pray for strength for me as I care for Heidi. Pray for the kids as they deal with the regular pressures of school and life while also worrying about their mom. Pray for emotional strength for all of us as we become weary in the fight. *Pray especially for Heidi to be healed of cancer.* We know that God is able to heal – that He is Good and that He is for us. Pray now that he would deliver Heidi from cancer. Let her/us know that you are praying for us (that is very encouraging!) Finally, each time we share answered prayers along the way, would you take a moment to Thank God and praise him (2 Corinthians 1:11). We need your prayers.

We appreciate all of you and the love and support we have received. We thank God for you! Blessings, Todd

August 26, 2014 – Update

So, tomorrow is Wednesday meaning Thursday is very close! Still not really thinking much about the reality of Thursday but thought I should call my Oncology Nurse just to ask some questions. I love my nurse, her name is Mary. When Mary and I first met, I thought she was a bit crazy... she told me in the sweetest voice, "Heidi, you are going to soar through Chemo" I thought, what? have you lost your mind? But Mary has been a great encouragement. She has let us share our lives with her, the story of our family and has grown to love and care for us. She always tells me of someone "like me" same age or same diagnosis and tells me how they are doing... it helps put things in perspective. Today, she told me one of her ladies was checking out after the same treatment I will get this week. She said she was tired but feeling well. I always hesitate to believe and then choose to say, great! I will just plan on that being me :)

She said our room is private and they are very nice. Almost made it sound like it would be vacation. She said the food it really good :) It will cost way more than vacation so we can try and pretend! I asked if I would be given the same daily medications I took before and she said yes. That alone will be the same as last time so I know at least I will feel somewhat cruddy until I am off those meds but they will take care of any nausea I would feel. Prefer cruddy to nausea... She explained a few other things but no daily shots until the blood is taken for my transplant, 3rd round of chemo, if I have that right. So, many details but for now, I am thankful for talking with her today, she is always honest, upbeat and caring. She helps calm fears!

She said I will hear from the hospital after 3 on Thursday and they will tell me my bed is ready and then we will just pack up and head out... sounds easy enough... so today I stayed home all day, when the storm rolled though I opened the windows, turned out the lights and just enjoyed the sound... it was so cool and so quiet in the house. God is caring for me for us and it will all be okay. Ready for 4 days of not cooking... got to look at the good things :) Blessings... Heidi

August 29, 2014 – Psalm 23:4

So, yesterday I was supposed to go into the hospital, never would have guessed I'd be sitting at home today. I think I've shifted all our schedule for the week. Pray all runs smoothly once we are actually at the hospital, yes, with me but also with the kids. It's hard to let go with tons of details and hope everything falls into place. I am so thrilled to find out that Kaitlin's teacher is a Christian and she was working over the summer at Chick-fil-a with Ashley, she said "it's her pleasure" to watch out for and help us care for Kaitlin at school this year. Just what a Mom needs to hear. God is good.

So, I sat yesterday at the car place getting my car checked so it works for Ashley this weekend. She offered to take me home but I knew going home would lead to my cleaning or doing something and I needed to sit. I started to read my book - *A Shepherd looks at Psalm 23* by W. Phillip Keller... It was given this last year and it's amazing that I was reading the chapter on verse 4 - yesterday. God knew. *"Even though walk through the valley of the shadow of death, (or "the darkest valley" – NIV) I will fear no evil, for You are with me, your rod and staff they comfort me."* That's my combo version... I sat reading, thinking of a couple of praise songs that I will post links to... one song came on the radio yesterday and Kaitlin said. "Mommy, this would be a good song to listen too when you have chemo." Such a sweet soft heart, one that understands our need for God and how music ministers to us.

This author spoke of how a shepherd leads its sheep through the valleys to get to the mountain top. It's too long to share, but he spoke of the long journey, how in the valley there was water for the sheep when they were thirsty, often in the valley is where we find literal refreshment from God. He speaks of how the shepherd knows the valleys, the lack of sun at times the dangers of animals, flash floods, rock slides etc. but although hard, difficult and dangerous at times the Shepherd knows this route is still the best way to lead them to high country. To the mountain top... He says "O God, this seems terribly tough but I know for a fact that in the end it will prove to be the easiest and gentlest way to higher ground."[16] Then when I thank him for the dark days, there He is in the midst, my panic, fear and misgivings give way to calm and quiet confidence in His care... Oh, there is just so much from just 7 pages in this book. He goes on to share how his wife actually lost her battle with cancer, I didn't see that coming and speaks of the lack of fear they had, the peace, God's presence with them. I honestly, struggled with the idea of saying, "God, thank you for cancer." It's such a strange struggle to thank God for pain for hard times... so contrary to what we would do or think... still struggling with that one.

With Christ there is no fear, there is calm. Today, I feel a bit stressed waiting but God holds the future. I realized through reading this chapter that we think death is NOT the norm! At least I realized I don't. I think everyone lives and some die... I mean who wants to think about death. Even when we hear someone has died, it hurts, it's sad, we say I'm so sorry... and then something about us wants to move away from it, because no one wants to really accept death as part of life. I smiled as I thought through this, it is kinda funny I think that we somehow think I'm fine, we are all fine... as if somehow we might be the one to escape death. Well, we all know that is not true. With life comes death... it's a harsh reality, one I don't like... so after saying that, I'm not going to suggest you take time to realize we all die, I'm just going to say, Live! Today, enjoy today but truth is although having cancer forces one to think of death, none of us is promised even one more breath. Each day a gift, each healthy day a gift, and today I'm thankful for more hours of feeling good. I have no idea why God is making us wait... but I'm thankful He is in control. I'm sad that my energy will be sapped and it's hard for me to talk and share face to face and while out in the community when I feel icky... but God uses all things and will continue. I am not down, hear me. I am thankful and just ready to get this round one behind us... I'm going to go to lunch with Kaitlin here soon, I enjoyed hearing about Max's first football game last night and they won - Go Merrillville! So much good, so much bad... we get to choose what we focus on.

> With Christ there is no fear, there is calm.

Know today if you are walking a hard path, it may not be cancer but I say, hard is hard, doesn't matter what it is... the list of hard is long! Don't fear, God is with you, He is your comfort! Love you all...[17]

August 30, 2014 – Good 1st day

So, we have been communicating details here and there and I'm finally going to put it all here :) Last night was a bit long, getting checked in late, then waiting for blood work before they could start chemo.

Chemo started at 12 a.m. - lovely... which made for a really long night of meds, more meds and then all the checks they do, at 5 a.m. they drew my blood again and then finally got to sleep! Yeah! They said they might put me on an IV drip because I'm dehydrated, which I didn't want because I need to sleep not pee every two seconds. When I work at 8:45, I was thankful to see the drip but they let me sleep and waited 'til morning to run the extra fluids. Thankful for those little things.

So, I woke up today feeling exhausted and a lingering headache but not sick. I have felt mostly myself today, however a bit of nausea tried to creep in this afternoon but some medicine took care of it. I got a long nap a partial shower... I asked "when can I shower? "she said you can't... not for 4 days... what? I told her that was not in the "brochure :)" My port is dual accessed and any water or anything getting into it can cause a blood infection, she said it happens a lot. Okay, so well then, I managed with the shower sprayer, very handy and the sink is big which allowed me to wash my hair and feel clean. Again, thankful for these little things... then Todd and I took a small walk for some fresh air and now wait for dinner to be served. Our "hotel" is nice... big flat screen, internet, games movies and room service 24 hours... thank God for that... I had to eat at 1:30 a.m. because when they keep you up all night you get really hungry.

As for my treatment. I only had one dose of chemo last night, I will receive that same dose tonight at 12 a.m. and then tomorrow night at 12 a.m. Tonight I will have a new drug at 1 a.m. it will take 1 hour. Then at 2 a.m. I will be set up on a 24-hour drip for another chemo. That will be it... after that 24 hours of fluid, putting me at discharge expected Tuesday. So, I am a bit concerned that tomorrow I will feel like I've been hit by a bus with the two new chemos tonight. I did have no major side effects from

last night but there is a long list I try not to read :) So, please pray that they are all minor... I still have an appetite so I have been trying to take advantage of the food and eat plenty, before that all changes. After discharge on Tuesday I will have to go get a shot... I do not have the name of it but I have heard about it. My nurse already suggested some medications to take after the shot. Our understanding is the shots are necessary to cause my bone marrow to produce more white blood cells since my body will be lacking them. They say this leads to your bones aching... so I hadn't been told any of that but I do believe a friend of mine went through those last year. Now you know why I don't read a lot and just take it one day at a time. Cannot worry about tomorrow... God is there and He will bring me through it and my supportive hubby, who I'm thankful to have by my side :) we are going to watch a movie tonight before tomorrow's craziness.

God is for us not against us! He loves us and in life or in death... it's all good.

Thank you for all the calls, e-mails, prayers and just everything you are all doing to make this whole process a bit easier and less stressful! God is caring for us each step of the way! Todd has his cell if you want to call, please feel free. Todd or I will try to keep you updated on how things are going... thanks again! Heidi

September 4, 2014 – After Chemo round #1

So, I can hardly believe a week has gone by since waiting to go the hospital, Wow! God has cared for us each step of the way. I will say the initial scheduling of it all and the rest of it was so stressful but God has sent many, each and every one of you to fill the gaps we have needed. Our kids cared for, meals (one from someone I don't even know, a friend of Todd's from the local coffee shop). We have seen God step in and take over details. We have had a few rough moments but God showed up there too and paved the way.

My care at the hospital was great and my feedback greater, apparently. I was told I was very articulate, well you have a lot of time to think of how care can be better. One way God showed up was after I discharged and had to get my shot, they said the wait was 2 hours... no way, I was not feeling well and needed to be home. Todd stepped in and talked to many people and they were able to have me in and out 30-45 minutes. I was able to share with the hospital today how this is not good care and a system needs to be set up so this just doesn't happen. The other situation led to extreme uncontrollable vomiting for a time... they let me manage my medication based on when I felt nauseous rather than staying ahead of the nausea, the good news is my Dr. was paged and called and helped us get it under control so I did not have to go right back to the hospital for fluids. I would have been very sad. Also, I believe this will not happen again, if different measures are taken next round! Thank God! I love that the hospital and Doctors listen. We had great nurses two, a couple favorites! Good care.

So, I am thankful that today I feel a bit stronger. That means I can move from the bed to the kitchen and the kitchen to the living room, resting in between. My body is very weak and feels it. I am however able to eat, after chemo diet for me is crazy... whatever looks or sounds good eat it... today that was Cheesecake dessert in the fridge and then I saw Chips and Salsa on TV and went and ate some of that... it's weird but tasted great! Praise God I have had NO dry mouth or sores, very pleased with that. I have had to adjust the air and get my fan back out... chemo throws you into hot flashes of some sorts... Oh, fun...

Each day I feel a little better and I am in good spirits, honestly. Yesterday was simple and I was still so sick but got to have one on one talking time with each one in my family. I was just thankful for that. I have kids who like to talk so Mom in bed means captive audience. I enjoy that time and the others I spoke on the phone with, just thankful. I did go to bed last night and couldn't sleep, Chemo meds do that to you... tired but wide awake and so I spent

Some time praying and a verse came into mind, so this morning I got out my Bible and Kate got up at 6:30 so I read Philippians 1:18-26 NIV

> *"And because of this I rejoice. Yes, and I will continue to rejoice, for I know that through your prayers and God's provision of the Spirit of Jesus Christ what has happened to me will turn out for my deliverance, I eagerly expect and hope that I will in no way be ashamed, but will have sufficient courage so that now as always Christ will be exalted in my body, whether by life or by death. For to me, to live is Christ and to die is gain. If I am to go on living in the body, this will mean fruitful labor for me. Yet what shall I choose? I do not know! I am torn between the two: I desire to depart and be with Christ, which is better by far; but it is more necessary for you that I remain in the body. Convinced of this, I know that I will remain, and I will continue with all of you for your progress and joy in the faith, so that through my being with you again your boasting in Christ Jesus will abound on account of me.*

Please don't read this and worry about me, I think it was a reminder, for me to live is Christ... I pray He is being made known and proclaimed through my life... and Paul understood that to die... was gain. I asked Kaitlin what does that mean? Mommy, it means it's okay if Paul dies because heaven is better... from the mouth of babes! I love when my kids hear and understand God's word and the truth that matters. God is *for* us not against us! He loves us and in life or in death... it's all good. Now, as I've said many times, I do believe it's God's plan for me to stick around...

I did have a moment when so sick and I said, "God I'm not strong enough to do this again." I know there will be those "horrific moments" as I like to call them. I'm sure I really don't know what that word really means but that's how they feel :) But I got through that moment and have to remind myself in those moments that I will get through, the pain or sickness will stop... I struggle for those to which my story is not their story. So much suffering and pain in this life... just reminded always that this is my story and someone is always in a worse situation. I will fight and push through and there will be those moments when I want to give up but I have much to live for... a friend dear to my heart told me her family is going to begin fostering a child and I loved it, got me so excited! Be inspired - Your life can make a difference! Allow God to work through you, no matter your situation. I love a new song I found "Hope in front of Me" there is always Hope when our lives rest in God... I couldn't do it any other way! Thankful for each day! Please do pray as I feel today is the beginning of my turn around time, felt a bit better, having some tingling in my legs, so please pray that subsides, not a side effect I'm going to like, kinda need to walk without my legs feeling strange and like they might not work... no pain from my shot though! So, a good day! A gift, each one... Heidi

Take the time to listen to this link so great a song... hope it works... Danny Gokey" Hope in Front of Me."[18]

September 8, 2014 – Monday Morning

So, a new week is upon me... the temperatures are cool and the sun is shining and I'm sitting at the kitchen table. Some physical progress has been made... but never as fast as I like. I think my biggest request at this time is to find a solution to the icky feeling that won't go away. My amazing nurse called me late last night to see how I was doing and to brain storm with me and seek to find solutions. I am always thankful for her. If I simply am not moving around I feel pretty good, I have regained much strength. In my mind how I feel is related to what I eat, so I continue to eat but doesn't seem to be helping how I feel. I did manage to go to church yesterday but only made it about 30 minutes before this heaviness set in and sickness... the world feels like a huge over-stimulating place still. My prayer is for a solution, 4 months of feeling this way will get increasingly challenging on a personal level. Driving or going to the store seems very overwhelming still.

So, today I will continue to be still and pray and think about all God is doing around me. I see Him working in the lives of those around me, I see Him working in the lives of my children. Just because life is not what we want it to be in the moment does not mean He is not at work. Life is not logical, it does not make sense, we so often want to put God in a box, because we simply can't understand. Well, He is God, He alone sees the Big picture, He is working things out for the good of me, because I am His child and He loves me. Faith is about believing, it's about action, not just words that fall by the wayside when life gets hard. A struggle for sure, but we are never alone.

Daily I am reminded to live for today! Tomorrow has enough trouble of its own... God has told us that. Be present in the moment, each moment. I believe in a world with tons of social media, we are very rarely present in the moment anymore. Always distracted. I challenge you today, set everything aside, be present in the moment with God, with your family, friends, with nature! Pay attention to all that is around you, don't miss it! Life is pretty amazing, even when it isn't going exactly the way we think it should, it's all perspective! What is yours? Make an amazing day! Heidi

September 14, 2014 – Update after Dr. visit

Well, I will start with some scripture I was reading this week. I just love 2 Corinthians... As I read 2 Cor.4:16-18 NKJV

> *Therefore we do not lose heart. Even though our outward man is perishing, yet the inward man is being renewed day by day. For our light affliction, which is but for a moment, is working for us a far more exceeding and eternal weight of glory, while we do not look at the things which are seen, but at the things which are not seen. For the things which are seen are temporary, but the things which are not seen are eternal.*

I think of the challenge to not lose heart... especially when we are reminded daily that this life is temporary. Even if the outward man is struggling, suffering whatever your case may be... in light of heaven and eternity... this life is but for a moment. The reality is as humans we just can't comprehend that, let's be honest. I know I can't. I live as if this life is it, if today is terrible then life is terrible, or hard or difficult. It is a constant struggle to be reminded that this is not it, if you know Christ. If you have a lasting, personal relationship with Him... don't lose heart. Paul of all people says "our light affliction" honestly some days don't seem so light and I don't think by reading

Faith is about believing, it's about action, not just words that fall by the wayside when life gets hard. A struggle for sure, but we are never alone.

about Paul his affliction from our perspective was light either... I think that's the key word... perspective. I think he was beginning to understand it is light, it is temporary and it is worth it. No matter who you are or where life finds you, God can use you!!!!!! No matter what, don't lose heart, on days you are down and discouraged, find HIM! He gets it, He has been there... He sweated drops of blood and asked God, if it be your will, please let this cup pass from me!" He understood pain and suffering, He did it all for us... and so our suffering in this life is hard and not fun and I'm prone to be like Jesus in saying "Please let this pass from me" but God has a bigger picture. Jesus' death was necessary to save you and save me... sometimes our pain is necessary, God does allow it... we can't see the bigger picture but we must not focus on what we can see but on the things we cannot. It's about trust, once again...

> No matter what, don't lose heart, on days you are down and discouraged, find HIM! He gets it, He has been there.

So, I went to the Dr. on Thursday and we had a great visit. He said he usually sees his patients very tired and he was kinda laughing that I was laughing and had managed to gulf down a black bean burger and fries in the office room while waiting on him. He was 1½ hours behind schedule, I was starved! He sat with us, as he always does as if he had nowhere to go, we asked tons of questions, some the same, over and over because it's always a lot to take in. He said with changing my nausea medications and taking away the pill we believe was making me sick, he anticipates me doing great this round! I always love their enthusiasm! My white counts were normal. Not normal for a person with cancer but NORMAL! He said the shot they gave me helped and they will continue them. I had no side effects from that shot, so that was great! Last time there was a lack of communication from discharge to me getting my shot and this round my Dr. and Nurse laughed and said, just wait and see what we are up to... not sure what that means but they are always working to give me the absolute best care. So thankful! When I go to stem cell, I will get a new team of Dr. and nurses, they said, "you are going to miss us." I agree! They are the best, so you can pray that my stem cell team is amazing too! You can pray that when I go into the hospital on Friday, the 19th... the medication changes keep me feeling well and managing everything other than being tired. I did sleep 2½ hours today, I could just feel the need. I did have a great week though!

I found myself excited each morning when I got out of bed and felt myself! Oh, something I have taken for granted too many times. I found myself tearing up in the car as I was driving to the store. Simply saying "thank you, God" ... I can drive and I feel well. A huge sense of contentment has filled me this week. Life is always so fast, so much all the time and mine stopped and then started again, slowly and it is refreshing to just take a deep breath... One of the great things so far this round of chemo... a huge praise... I have been able to focus, even though I was sick. Last time, I was always over-stimulated. I would lay in bed, unable to watch TV or read anything, I just couldn't handle it. Even when I felt my worst this time, when I was in bed I felt okay. I have enjoyed reading my Bible, my book, and just relaxing and watching some TV... having very few moments of feeling over-stimulated. So, I would ask for prayers for that to continue. Chemo brain... well, not sure when it hit me last time but it's a very real thing... hoping to not get hit too hard with it.

So, yesterday I stopped in Kohl's and as I was checking out I had this moment of realizing, I look normal to all those around me. No one would even consider I am sick... but this week I will shave my head. I planned on Friday but as of yesterday I have lost about half of my hair... so Monday or Tuesday will be the day. It's a reality that even though we don't ever plan on starring, we look at others different and my world will change a bit in a few days. Hair is simply the outward sign to others that I am sick, I think that is one of the struggles of a bald head, it makes its own statement. Honestly, I am fine with it. Sure I might have a moment but I might not... at this point, it is what it is... I will begin looking different every time people see me, long blonde hair, short brown hair, just a hat, it's really whatever I feel that day, does add variety to life :) Thank you all for the many prayers, cards and meals! They are each a blessing! We are so very thankful! Round #2 will be behind us soon! Let's get this done :) Love you all! Heidi

September 21, 2014 – Day two chemo...

So, my 4:30 a.m. labs and meds and blood pressure have me awake. I thankfully got a stretch of about 6 hours of sleep last night. Always feels so long when I am here. We got checked in late on Friday night so my chemo did not get started 'til Saturday 12... later than I wanted but again, you have to just be a long for the ride, can't control any of it. I am asking for prayers today because I went to bed feeling emotionally weak last

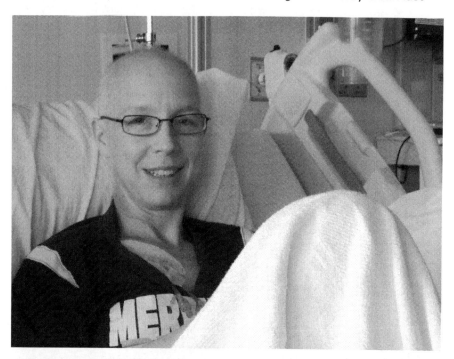

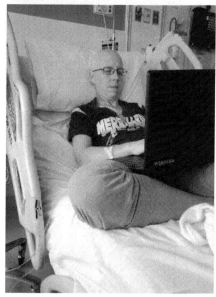

night. Only the first day and lots of extra medications to keep me from getting nauseous but lots of meds make you feel icky. My appetite stops once chemo starts so already struggling a bit with that. I have a few other physical things going on that are not helping, including mild headaches... that is beginning to subside, thankfully. So, my nurse said "stay positive, it's going to be a good day." I will try, just hate feeling ick all the time and have to admit, ick brings on some anticipatory nausea and bad memories from last round. Praying it's not a really long day! That's all I've got, thanks! Heidi

September 24, 2014 – Thank you

I want to start by saying thank you for continued prayers! We have had amazing family and friends come along side and care for our kids. I have not worried about my children and that is a huge blessing! We have had food dropped off and made for us. We have an amazing support system and we are so very thankful.

I don't think I would have made it through yesterday without your prayers. Not sure what was going on but I felt a bit like that song "I feel like a Monster" like if they didn't let me out of the hospital I might just lose it a bit. I waited 'til 2 to finish my fluids, 'til 3 for discharge papers, then transportation, then my shot, then the valet, then drive through for dinner and then traffic, finally to my home sweet home around 6 p.m. I felt this building inside like I just wanted to scream, for it all to be over, to just be home. Honestly, it wasn't that bad, just a sense of discontent inside this round... a struggle, I couldn't seem to get to go away. So, I ask that you begin praying now for next round and more importantly the 2-3 weeks in November that we anticipate... it is a long time. I imagine I will be very sick and tired and honestly, that will help. No shower, probably over 50 pills to swallow, in the last 5 days... yuck, the smells - soap, sanitizer, the alcohol, the food smells... just ewww! Sometimes you just want to run... God has cared for me though and I am really okay. There are just those moments where you look in the mirror or you feel really sick and your brain reminds you of reality - I have cancer! What? how did that happen, how did we get here. I think I deny a lot in order to keep going, I just get through... so pray that I continue to plug away. That God provides the mental sanity necessary to push through.

I did meet a really sweet lady when waiting for my shot, she asked right out, what do you have? She was diagnosed with Breast Cancer in April 2013, me Hodgkin's Feb 2013, she was just re-diagnosed, me too... She encouraged me and said "stay strong." Helps to know you are not alone. I overheard a women saying her husband had a transplant in May and was now on 4 of his 17 more chemo treatments. In that moment, I thank God, that's not me... I can't imagine that many more.

I was reading at the hospital in my book and she said, "God DOES give us more than we can handle."[19] I agree with her, I don't believe the scriptures teach God won't give us more than we can handle. Often life is too much. Without more than we can handle... we handle it on our own. We need God and He provides strength for the journey. Not always the journey I want to be on but He will provide. So, I simply ask for continued prayers to enjoy every day and strength for the hard ones. I did get a blood transfusion this round, my hemoglobin is higher than it's probably ever been. I've always had low counts. So, once I get past this initial ick... I should have more energy. The bad medication from last round was dropped and my nausea meds have been done well, leaving no room for vomiting! Yeah!!! So, back to one day at a time until the ick passes... thanks for reading, and praying! We love and appreciate you all! No One Fights Alone![20] Heidi

September 30, 2014 – Post round #2

I am happy to say this has been the best round yet. I have been very "chemo" tired which is going to take some getting used to but I was able to attend church on Sunday and even go out of the house, driving myself and spending time with Kate on Saturday. That was a great feeling! I feel like life is a bit in slow motion, my days start late. Today, I am just getting out of bed and it's going on 1 p.m. I just felt the need to stay in bed and sleep and I think I made the right call. Chemo sleepy, means, if I sit, I might fall asleep, just a gentle drifting off to sleep - on the couch or the back porch or if I try to read it lasts only a short time. I sometimes feel my body is kinda lifeless, just weighs nothings, like I'm floating on clouds and could just do that all day :) If I only felt this way in the hospital but the chemo drugs cause antsy, restlessness, being awake while the body is tired and it's just icky. As I write this though I'm thinking this after - sleepiness may be the thing that helps me through the extended time in the hospital in November... Hmmmmmm

God continues to care for us and for that I'm thankful. I do feel myself struggling a bit. Adjusting to no hair again has been weird. I bought cute bandanna's and that may be my new look, I love my hats but a visor always makes me feel like something is between me and the other person when I speak. The bandanna's keep my head warm and are quite comfy :) Who knew bandanna had two n's in it? I think I need to go back to school. I do love my wig and did wear it on Sunday, so nice to feel myself a bit but not practical for my everyday life.

It looks like Friday the 3rd will be my checkup/ blood work and a bunch of tests. Waiting to see if my PET and CT's will get scheduled, if not they will add another day to our schedule. These all day visits are hard to manage with all our craziness. A nurse also called with 3 more tests I need to have pre- my transplant. Gee, no one mentioned those... don't seem like a big deal, just take all day. One I do need prayers for though.

Apparently, they will check my veins. They will be seeing if they can handle the Mobilization (the taking of my cells for transplant and placing them back) if they can that would be GREAT! if not, I am told I have to have one small procedure to put a line in... what? no one mentioned that. It's just a minor surgery, so I'm told... I'm thinking so another day to put it in, and another day to take it out... Yikes. At this point it's all a bit overwhelming, sure I feel like it's going rather fast but I feel my mental stamina lacking a bit. Just wanting to be on the other side and lots of wondering as to what they are really going to do to me :) I am confident God will bring me through, just ready to be through! Ever been there? So, it's almost one and I have enjoyed some great Fall things today, both a Carmel Apple and a Pumpkin donut! It's been a good day! Better see if I can shower and get dressed before Kate gets home from school, always the goal :) Have a great day!

October 8, 2014 – Update

So, I have been waiting to update but many are asking so I will give you what I have... My scans were very good but borderline for whether or not I could skip my 3rd chemo. They planted the seed but said they would have to wait for the final Radiologist's reading. The reading left my Dr. saying I need to do the last chemo. We, of course, want no chance or the best chance of the cancer not returning so the 3rd chemo we will do. I was scheduled for this week but it will be delayed until next week. We are assuming it will be Wednesday due to other time sensitive things in regards to my treatment.

If I have chemo on Wednesday that will leave me with me getting my stem cells "mobilized" – collected on probably Monday the 27th... they are collected when my counts come back, usually 12 days after treatment. After mobilization they will wait about a week and then I will be hospitalized... for my final blast of chemo followed by the stem cell transplant. We are looking at possibly the 4th of November... today my team is having a meeting at 4:30 so I am told it will be tomorrow before they have a schedule and approvals etc. that are needed. The transplant also involves a bunch of other things like a vein check. I will get that done while in the hospital. You can pray that my veins can handle collection, if not I will have to have a minor procedure to place a line in my chest for this... not too excited about that. However, if needed they said I will get it placed while in the hospital next week, so that would make one day go a bit faster than just lying around. I think I had such a hard time last time because the steroids make you a little jittery, antsy, you want to go and do, be moving while at the same time you don't feel well. A lack of patience is involved :) I also have to have a bunch of shots and meds but I'm confident at this time that Todd will do a great job. I got a flu shot and barely felt the shot, I think it will be about the same.

I will continually say that I know God is caring for us. My Dr. said I am responding really great to treatment! He continues to say this and when my counts bounce back I feel really well. I still get tired and have to make myself rest but for the most part I feel "normal" ... I also continue to see God take care of the details that are over and over... overwhelming! This weekend we had a lot packed in with the kids and my being in round 3 and now, I'm not doing it this weekend. I'm thankful we will be home to manage a busy weekend and also for the extra days to feel well. We continue to have many people offering help and so many sending notes, messages, food... just caring for us!

I will ask for prayers for God to provide someone to help for November and December with transportation of one of our children at least one way for school. It is about a 25-minute commute. This is a door God opened before cancer and now we will trust Him to provide a way... Pray for Todd... I can't imagine being in the hospital for 2-3 weeks and part of that is survival mentally for me and the other is how will life work without me here? Again, God has provided and we will be on the other side soon but the strength, momentum and just planning is overwhelming... "When my heart is overwhelmed... lead me to the ROCK that is higher than I" ... Psalms 61:2. God can handle it all, I, We cannot! So we trust Him with each day. It's hard, I won't lie to you... I cried a bit when my Dr. said I had to do the 3rd round. I knew he was going to say it but so hoped just a little he wouldn't.

Enjoying each day, hugs from Max, Ashley smiling in the front row at her concert last night... having a good time. The conversations I am blessed to have daily with Bailey and Sabrina and the spiritual growth I see and pray for in each of our children. The snuggle time with Kate, who has that on her list to do today :) A husband who is beside me each and every step and family and friends who have been amazing. I had someone say to me today – "your family has an amazing support system, we just don't see that very often!" We are blessed, thank you for being a part of the journey! Heidi

October 17, 2014 – update

Hello, everyone! I have no idea what I updated last and no time to read and find out so here it goes... Sunday the 19th I will go in for my #3 chemo... I have bed priority so they tell me due to my transplant schedule. Please still pray that I get a bed on Sunday and earlier than later so they can get my meds and start on Sunday. Laying around 'til Monday and waiting is a long process. The amount of details that go into planning for these times away is a mess... God has given us so much help but daily it seems schedules change and that becomes overwhelming fast when you are relaying that to those helping and those not familiar with your normal. After chemo I will have my Neulasta shot before leaving the hospital again, never a fast process and always requires lots of patience which is hard when you are pumped with steroids. Pray for that process. Due to the timing of all this, I do not have to have the at home shots for several days, we get to skip that, Yeah! One small silver lining. The following week I will get blood drawn Mon/Tues to watch my counts the prayer is that my counts are good and ready on Wednesday for mobilization (sitting at the hospital for 3-5 hours while they take my blood to freeze for transplant) if they do not get what they need on Wed I come back on Thurs... pray they get it all on Thursday! Then hospitalization for transplant is scheduled for November 4th. I will get 6 days of Chemo and then on Day 7 the transplant will occur! Then 10-12 days of recovery, in the hospital! Sounds simple right? Everything for transplant is dependent on the thing before it's all timed, so pray all runs as planned. Pray for peace. I feel not stressed about all I have just written, just stress about all we do on a daily basis and all the kids being cared for... I know they are cared for well, but there are a lot of steps in our house on a daily basis. I'm sure once I am in the hospital all will be fine and I will focus on me, just hard to think about being away for 3 weeks... a few days okay but three weeks, yikes! I am confident that God will bring us through and confident all will go well! Just pray for rest, strength for the whole family and all those helping! Thanks, gotta run, long list of to do's plus some needed rest in there before Sunday! Heidi

October 24, 2014 – post 3rd Chemo...

As I laid in bed watching 12 a.m. approach I realized all my extra sleep and medications have caught up with me. I even took something to help me sleep and still wide awake at 12:48... so hoping sometime soon I will be able to sleep. I will say my day started by my being frustrated at how tired I was and now I end not tired at all! I slept 'til 12 noon but after the kids started strolling in and I got up and moving it was a really good day! The weather was a beautiful Fall day, kids played outside, visited with neighbors and had a few wonderful ladies stop by with food! Always a huge - thank you! I was able to spend quality time with Todd and all the kids today, a good day!

As I lay awake thankful tonight I struggle with the thoughts of days ahead. My hospital stay makes me a bit crazy! Something about feeling trapped a bit, always being hooked up to something, food doesn't taste good after day one, and you just don't feel well and honestly don't want to do anything. But there is this antsy feeling inside from all the medications that makes you want to move, go, do but you can't because you are too stimulated. The TV is on, but no volume for me. I stare at the computer and my eyes get so sleepy...

Todd and I played a game of cards and I got frustrated because I simply couldn't make a decision about what to play... the brain just kinda shuts down. I am thankful for the many prayers that helped us get home on Wednesday night as we had wanted. It was 11:30 p.m. but we got home and for that I was thankful! Today I noticed I felt bruised, a strange kind of feeling all over my body... then it hit me... it's the pain they mentioned from my shots... but thankfully it's not pain, just discomfort, kinda like you whole body is a bruise, so no touching or hugging...

So, I think my biggest struggle right now is trying to mentally come up with a plan to survive 21 days in the hospital, the first 6 being the worst because I will be hooked up to fluids and chemo meds... I seriously need a plan. Prayers will be the foundation and then more on top of that. I am told there is a girl named Bridget who helps us through this time, she works with physical therapy and will teach us to knit even... this may be necessary! I know God will get me through, at this time, I don't know how because it feels very overwhelming... next week's details feel overwhelming. Blood work M/Tues and then if my counts are good they will mobilize my blood on Wednesday. My veins are good enough for that. I was told so no tube yet, not until the transplant, if all goes as well.

Again, always so thankful for those who are caring for us behind the scenes at in the front row... we have so many details and they make me very stressed especially when Dr. and Nurses say changes can be made and we just have to adjust. Very stressful! So please continue to pray for just good days! Good moments with family! I really cherish each one! Pray for a plan to get through, a peace that I know only God can give. I didn't do so well with even 3 days so a bit worried about 3 weeks. We did have amazing nurses, one who shared how special Todd and I were to some of them on the floor. Seeing our love and support of one another. People are always watching and God gave great opportunity for us to share our story with that nurse! I never doubt God is working, just always selfishly wondering how I will survive it all and keep my sanity. God is bigger than this all and even if I do lose my mind, My God is able to restore it :) We will hope it doesn't come to that... Transplant still scheduled for November 4, 2014... Heidi

October 28, 2014 – Prayers needed

So, yesterday and today I got my blood drawn to see when and if my counts are up and ready for me to go get my blood taken for transfusion. The answer is no. They anticipate it will take a few more days. I had anticipated this from the beginning. I know my body and have been aware of when my counts are down and then all of a sudden I feel great the next day, the day they bounce back. Well, I will say today I feel tired. So, I am going to ask that you pray my counts jump today for tomorrow's blood draw. My nurse said they will likely not be able to draw on Thursday and that means if we wait 'til Friday... there is a good chance all will not be complete for an admission on November 4th as planned. It's not like anything has gone as planned and as frustrated as it has all been, in the end it all usually works out just fine. Planning for 3 weeks though is so much and it would just be amazing if God would allow things to go as planned this one time :) If not, we will trust that His plan is better, His plan is perfect and there is some reason but it's all just a lot! So, I'm going to eat lunch and rest and then wrap as many Christmas gifts as I can get done :) Yes, I'm about done shopping. Even Christmas has to be planned ahead this year! We don't know what tomorrow ever holds, we plan and pray and trust God to bring us through! Thankful for this amazing weather this week, it has been an added blessing! Have a great day and thanks for all your prayers, we will see what Gods' plan is :) Heidi

October 29, 2014 – Fear and Worry

As I got started for my day today, there seemed to be a bit of fear lingering. I'm not sure where it came from but I have a good guess. As I sat on the couch snuggling with a crying 9-year-old last night, she said, "Mommy, what if it comes back? Mommy, what if?" I think the thoughts of a small child, their words often mirror our own fears and worries. To think what it would be like to be 9 and worried if Mommy will be sick, mommy will be gone for 21 days... it's hard as a parent. I want to say, I will be fine but reality is we never know what tomorrow holds, not me... not you! We hope in Christ, We pray for healing, we press on, we plan, we do... Yesterday I read in Matthew 6, speaks of MY Heavenly Father knowing what I need... sometimes we question that, we question "then why are you not doing or allowing this God?" I'm all about being honest. I am human, flesh, dust... frail. We all struggle and God can handle it, really! Therefore, do not worry about tomorrow... I thought "okay God," yesterday and then today, fear creeps in... many of my fears are not even related to the present. I think I have a peace about transplant and know God will bring us through it. I think a lot of the fear is of the future. Fear of cancer, again. Frustration about having no control over schedule. Thankful in the next breath for days I am feeling well and then angry that I am an emotional wreck on those good days!

Today... Isaiah 41:9-13 ESV

> You are my servant, I have chosen you and not cast you off"; Fear not, for I am with you; be not dismayed, for I am your God; I will strengthen you, I will help you, I will uphold you with my righteous right hand... For I, the Lord your God, hold your right hand; it is I who say to you "Fear not, I am the one who helps you"

There are times God chooses us. Today, I do not really want to be chosen to struggle – To be an example. Thankful though that my foundation is firm in Christ. That is never shaken. Thankful the God of the universe will hold my hand.

We have things we want in this life, honestly each day even... and when we don't get it, we struggle, we are frustrated. Big and small. I think I am just struggling like Paul, asking God to take this from me. I pray this will be the last time I hear the word cancer. I pray God will not choose this as a continued journey for our lives. It's hard.

Don't get me wrong, Cancer is just one of many hard things in this life. We all do hard at some level, hard for us... don't feel because I have not had Cancer I can't relate... God brings us to the end of ourselves, sometimes over and over. He wants to know that I can and will accept this path He has chosen for me but I am still working on that... I pray that others will and do see Christ in me but it's all God... because the battle is real. I want many things in this life and no one stops wanting stuff in this life just because they are sick. We all have hopes, dreams... What does God want for me though? not sure on many days... not thinking we are on the same plan... since I'm struggling. He wants faithfulness, trust...

So, pray for peace that I need to not live life in fear, really just moments in fear... pain, sickness, abuse, addiction, suffering, death, all parts of life, all parts I don't like. Thankful that someday God will put an end to all this, thankful for His victory on the cross that guarantees me and You if you seek and follow Him by trusting in His love and forgiveness of your sins on the cross. I long for Revelation 21:4 ESV *"He will wipe away every tear from their eyes, and death shall be no more, neither shall there be mourning, no crying, no pain anymore, for the former things have passed away."* I long for this and I'm thankful that I know who holds my future, I know my home is in Heaven, I KNOW! If you don't know... ask someone who has this personal relationship with Christ. Ask me... I cannot live without it! I may not have answers to everything in this life, but God does. He loves me, He cares for me and He will walk beside me, us - through it all! Thanks for listening - Heidi

October 30, 2014 – A stressful day so far... (Todd)

We're at the hospital today for collection of stem cells– on track for final intense chemo and stem cell therapy beginning Tuesday (a three-week hospital stay) – then, Lord willing, we're done with cancer.

Right now, they are having a difficult time getting her started and the anxiety is adding to the mix. Pray that they are able to get the lines in without further difficulty. Pray today for her strength as the collection process is pretty draining. Also that they get all they need today so she doesn't have to come back tomorrow.

November 1, 2014 – Tears and anxiety

So, this week was a long one. Longer than I expected. I try not to "know" too much going into things. Most procedures/chemo's etc. are limited, a day or two of sickness or discomfort. I think I'm really having a hard time wrapping my head around next week. Really it's just a few days away. After this week experiences, about 19 needles in a few days and bruised arms, apparently I am not great at relaxing and breathing. Thank God for medication. I felt okay last night was able to take Kate out in the horrible weather to trick or treat for about an hour then get ice cream. The night ended with her sad and worried and crying in my lap and me too. Reality is here and although you work hard to force the negative thoughts away they are working hard... although you try to relax and accept, the body apparently knows what is coming.

Today, a pit in my stomach, my heart feels like it's racing a bit and won't stop. I had hoped to just feel good, get the house cleaned and stuff done but the process is slow today. I am thankful for very patient nurses who got me through the collection of my stem cells. God has been faithful in that. When you are the "special situation" they refer to other nurses about well, gotta love those moments. But we got through. I need much prayers for entering the hospital on Tuesday for starters, I will have a line put in, so we don't have to do what we did the last few days, so hopefully I will be sedated for the first day of chemo to lighten the stress. I keep telling myself by next Sunday the worst will be over... it's true chemo will be done and Monday will be transplant, then recovery. I realize I'm good at getting through today or a few days but endurance I may not be so good at. I have to re set my mind and Wow, it's super hard. Then there are the fears of what if it doesn't work, what if I get an infection, what if, well, let's not say my worst fear. This is scary stuff, just being honest. I keep thinking this round of tears will be the last but don't seem to be. So, I'm asking God to wrap His arms so tightly around me I feel Him! Asking Him to hold me and carry me through, because I simply don't know how to do this part of the journey.

> I'm asking God to wrap His arms so tightly around me I feel Him! Asking Him to hold me and carry me through, because I simply don't know how to do this part of the journey.

Breathe, that is what they keep telling me, I have done a lot of that and plan to do a lot more. Pray for complete healing. My Dr. said cure Is only 50%, now you know why I don't read stuff they tell me to read and I don't listen. Who wants to hear that when they are going through all this. Five years with a clean PET indicates cure as to remission. I have to trust and I do although this is the hardest thing I've ever done... no one gets to do it for you, only walk beside you. I'm thankful for y'all! Now if the butterflies in my stomach and racing heart would just stop. Thank you all for taking this journey with us, I hope I'm not to open for your comfort. Believe me I left a lot of things I would typically say out just from my experiences this week. Thankful for the medical field and all they do but it is not a fun process and my heart goes out to all who have walked this path or one similar... hard stuff. Heidi

November 3, 2014 – Tomorrow

So, I keep asking myself, how does one prepare mentally for the most difficult thing they have ever had to do? We have things in life, we avoid, we run from, people we avoid, jobs we might quit because it's too hard or whatever the circumstance. I am reminded that we don't always get a choice about whether to do HARD or run away and choose another route. Some things like sickness and death are just present. Sure, I could choose another route, not doing treatment but that would not accomplish the hoped end goal - Cure. I hear songs like Mandisa's "Overcomer" or Jamie Grace's "Fighter" and I think, "how is that me? I don't feel strong, I feel weak." I think God has a scripture for us in that department (2 Corinthians 12). His grace is enough, we sing it, do we believe it, do I believe it? I have to say all Glory goes to HIM! When I think of where my life has come from and struggles I had in my 20's with depression, I never could have handled any of this then... God taught me to trust and sure, I never imagined I would have to do it at this level, never. I assure you I am doing nothing. God is leading the way. The God of Angel Armies, is by MY side! I don't know if it's appropriate to say but a passage of scripture keeps flooding my mind. I keep thinking of Jesus in His humanity. His brokenness, His feeling of being overwhelmed, His time praying to His Father before the hardest toughest journey He ever took (His death on the cross for me). He asked His disciples to Pray (and I thank you for your prayers and not falling asleep on me :) – Matthew 26:36-45. He was mentally preparing Himself for what was ahead. *"If it is possible, may this cup be taken from me. Yet not as I will, but as you will..."* How hard to say that... life is full of Hard, the worst kind and it's so hard to understand... I don't understand it but I am confident that tomorrow I will put one foot in front of the other and face my current biggest fear.

His grace is enough, we sing it, do we believe it, do I believe it?

From reading above I will ask you to pray as you feel led, I don't know how to ask specifically. I'm not sure I even have the ability to process all of my emotions. But some specific requests I have are this (1) Pray for minimal side effects. How bad they are will determine my strength. Weight has been a minor issue with just 3 days in the hospital, being sick for 3 weeks could leave me wiped out. I need to be able to eat. (2) Pray for wonderful patient nurses! God has been faithful in that so far. (3) Pray for our lives to be a testimony to those who care for us. (4) Pray for me to keep my thoughts positive even on hard days and my mind busy or resting. (5) Pray for Todd. He will be supporting me and that is not an easy job :) and also commuting back and forth some of the time. (6) Pray for our children. It's hard for a Mom to leave her kids when they too must

be struggling with the reality of all that is going on. Pray that they will have the support they need and be distracted and the time will go quickly. (7) Oh, one last major one is infection. Dr. seemed most concerned about that which could prolong my hospital stay or land me in ICU. (Doctors really shouldn't tell their patients all these worrisome things, just their husbands) I am thankful for Todd, he has not left me alone for anything! He has been amazing and I know I couldn't have come through all this so far and can't do the next 3 weeks alone. Pray he too stays healthy. (8) I go in tomorrow at 11 a.m. I will have minor surgery at 12. I hate these minor surgeries. Doesn't help I can't eat tomorrow either because of it. Pray it runs smoothly and not much pain from the insertion of a line of some sort for the transplant.

One thing that I would ask, as a Mom! If you know my kids, and see them. Love on them for me! Hug them, ask them how they are, pray with them! Our address is *****. Would you write them personal notes or send them verses to encourage them? If you don't know them they are Ashley, Sabrina, Bailey, Max and Kaitlin. Receiving something personal would encourage and brighten their days. Many of you have been faithful in sending cards to me and I so thank you but if you would love on them, it would mean so much.

I would also ask that if we are Facebook friends, will you fill my FB page with encouraging stuff. Verses, funny things you read or watch, positive quotes. A favorite song of yours, that I can just listen to in bed. I believe that could be a great way to help me pass time and if I'm not feeling up to skimming FB Todd can do it for me. I love personal messages too! We make an amazing team! Thanks, we could not do this without you! Heidi

November 4, 2014 – Ending day 1

So, today went well My surgery was okay, always have to wait a long time but it's done and over I am a bit sore and will need a few days to heal. Small insertion in my chest to run a line for the transplant They are also able to run my chemo off of it, so kinda a bonus. I don't have to be hooked up on both sides, just one. I am currently getting my first chemo now, unable to stay away for more than about 10 minutes, must be from all of today's medication but that's okay, it helps to get good rest when I am able. I do feel like when explained all that will happen the next weeks it seemed less scary. My nurse said I should not really feel the effects of the chemo over the next few days. The steroids likely yes, but all the norms, nausea, vomiting etc. Mostly the same concerns and hopefully medication will help. She did mention though on Sunday I will receive the worst dose. That one has many side effects that they work hard to minimize. Something about eating ice chips for 6 hours straight to ward off mouth sores... not sure, guess I'll know when Sunday comes. She also mentioned the side effects are not typically immediate. From the Sunday dose, it will be 4-7 days after my transplant next Monday before the side effects will be in full force, due to my immunity system being at its lowest. But it's only days she said. So, for me, it's back to one day at a time. I'm quite content tonight. Todd asleep, since the time change and busy schedule he got about 3 hours of sleep last night. Pray he stays rested and well to care for me. Pray for my pain from surgery to stop quickly and for it to heal fast and well, no infections. I was able to eat a full meal today around 5:30 after no food all day, so that was a praise. It is the little things most days! Pray I will just be at ease and content here. They have a little concert tomorrow, something about a cello player and someone else coming to play music for an hour. God will bring distractions, help me to do them, feel well enough and be able to pass the time. Day one is winding down... thank you all for your support! Chemo round one is done, just beeped! We will see what tomorrow holds. Oh, another praise, I do not have to be hooked up to IV all the time. All my chemo's run about 3 hours Max and then I get a break. My nurse does not believe I will have to have any round the clock fluids. So less peeing and more ability to move around freely. These two small things are amazing - if you are me :) Might even get a shower before a week... don't take those little things for granted :) Night - Heidi

November 6, 2014 – Day 3 chemo

So, last night I began to feel icky around 5ish. I got some meds and then basically slept all night and through to the morning. I thought today would be followed by more icky and was thankful to wake up feeling well. I ate my breakfast, thankful for that. I checked my weight, it is maintained so far. The little things matter. I then got on my tennis shoes and went and walked on the treadmill for only 20 minutes but it felt good. Sat and looked at a magazine. Now I am in bed hooked up to the first of today's chemo. My chemo will run from 10-2 a.m. and then 10-2 p.m. today through Saturday. Sunday they say will be the worst. Something about 6 hours of sucking on ice chips to keep my mouth and esophagus from terrible sores. This will also allow for infection which they will keep a very close eye on. Please pray for minimal side effects. Getting out of the side effects does not seem to have been presented as an option. They will be there, just how good or bad will be determined. So, lots of prayers appreciated and no infection. Also timing of some of those are really important. Things have to be "checked" for infection and if during the day, I can have access to results quickly and medications if needed but if trouble in the evening when those resources are closed for the night I will have to basically suffer 'til morning. So, please pray for timing... side effects should not be immediate they are saying the 14-17th will be my worst days after transplant.

Thank you all so much for your messages, it gives me great joy to hear from you, to be able to respond to you, just gives me stuff to do when I am feeling okay. It's wonderful! Keep it up! Today I was reading some stuff on the whole cancer/suicide Brittany Maynard responses.[21] I was reading some stuff by Piper and Joni Eareckson Tada... Verses I really like are 1 Corinthians 6:19 *"Do you not know that your bodies are temples of the Holy Spirit, who is in you, whom you have received from God? You are not your own;"* We are not our own. Reminder that God is God, we are His, I am not my own. Our lives are not our own, our children's and loved one's lives are not our own. Such a hard concept to grasp at times. A good reminder. God has a purpose for each waking moment, each hour. Our lives touch and affect others up until our last breath... others lives affect my life! Loving, serving... each other, this is no one-way street. I also like 2 Corinthians 1:8 NIV

> *We do not want you to be uninformed, brothers and sisters, about the troubles we experienced in the province of Asia. We were under great pressure, far beyond our ability to endure, so that we despaired of life itself.*

Paul acknowledges troubles, great pressure, having to deal with things we feel we can't endure... despairing even of life at times... We must rely on the God who raises the dead. 2 Corinthians 1:9-11 NIV,

> *Indeed, we felt we had received the sentence of death. But this happened that we might not rely on ourselves but on God, who raises the dead. He has delivered us from such a deadly peril, and he will deliver us again. On him we have set our hope that he will continue to deliver us, as you help us by your prayers. Then many will give thanks*

on our behalf for the gracious favor granted us in answer to the prayers of many.

HE delivers us and will deliver us again, our hope is in Him, and YOU ALL are helping by your prayers. You are loving, serving, ministering to us and we give great thanks! 2 Corinthians 4:16-18 NIV

Therefore we do not lose heart. Though outwardly we are wasting away, yet inwardly we are being renewed day by day. For our light and momentary troubles are achieving for us an eternal glory that far outweighs them all. So we fix our eyes not on what is seen, but on what is unseen, since what is seen is temporary, but what is unseen is eternal.

*** And these I love too... we are all wasting away, in our flesh YET, if we know Christ in a real and personal way he is renewing us each day! Our troubles don't feel light and momentary, I think what Paul is saying is that compared to eternal glory, Heaven will far outweigh all the pain and suffering on this each. I will try to remember that this week as I suffer through some tough things physically but if I fail in the moment, God's grace will be enough to pull me through with all your support.

**** I will close with this final scripture I found today also... Romans 14:7-8 NIV

For none of us lives for ourselves alone, and none of us dies for ourselves alone. If we live, we live for the Lord; and if we die, we die for the Lord. So, whether we live or die, we belong to the Lord.

So the question is, do you belong to the Lord? Have you committed your life, your every breath to Him? Not do you just know who Jesus is but have you accepted Him as your personal Savior? His death, His resurrection, Have you sought His forgiveness and vowed to follow Him with your life and in your death? Know for sure that when you die you will see Your Savior, face to face, no doubts, no regrets, Only Jesus. Only He can cover our sins, it's not about who we are or what we have done, only what He has done... sent Jesus to die once for all, have you accepted Him as your Savior? Only these great things, comfort, promises, love, community of believers comes from the Lord! He alone brings peace, Hope, strength... okay I will be done for now. Thanks for continued prayers... each day I am feeling it and keep it up because the hardest days are coming but I am confident, I know who goes before me, I know who stands behind, the God of angel Armies is by my side! He has brought an army of believers and friends to care for us and we could not be in better hands! We press on... Heidi

November 7, 2014 – Day 4

Today was not as good as yesterday but I can't complain. My white cell count dropped some, as is expected, so might be the cause of a feeling a little crummy. My blood pressure and weight have remained good. My appetite took a bit of a plunge today but I still ate most of two meals. I did not sleep all that well last night, lots of people in and out all night. I get my 2nd round of chemo each day from about 10 p.m. 'til 2, then vitals every 4 hours so in and out they come. I did get blood today as well, so my red cells should be higher tomorrow and possibly give me a bit more energy. I took a small walk today with Todd. Thankful to not be here alone. Today I started reading a story of a young girl who just a month ago has something attack her body, she is in Comer's Hospital right up here next to me. She is only 12 and her name is Kaitlyn. She has suffered much more tragic and scary things than I have as I read her story, her family continues to fight for and with her in a very scary situation. She has been lost almost all function of her body and they are seeing daily improvements but her story has given me the reminder that someone always has it worse than you do. Even when life is hard there are others in similar situations, crisis, living moment by moment, depending on Dr, Nurses, family and those supporting them in prayers. So, I ask you to pray for sweet Kaitlyn. I imagine I would rather suffer than to watch my child go through such a tough thing and have no means to do anything for them. They are a family of faith and I know God is giving them strength for each day as well. So, as I look at the next week of treatment and not knowing fully what to expect, I am just thankful. Thankful for today. For so much! Knowing and trusting God has a plan and even when we can't understand it, He has not lost control! So, my day has not been fantastic but it has gone fast and I have endured and for that I am thankful Todd is off to pop popcorn and we are putting a movie on. Day 4 has come and gone and I'm ready for day 21 to come quickly so I can see my family again. Looks like some may get to come visit tomorrow, so again. Just praying for a good day and then another and thankful for the care of good nurses! We are in good hands! Thank you for continued prayers! We know they are working and remember, prayers for minimal side effects, I would really appreciate! Night all! Heidi

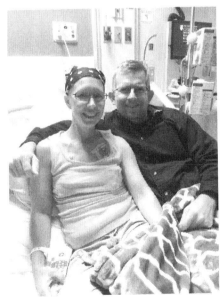

November 10, 2014 – Stem cell transplant done

So, today was the day. It was really quite uneventful. Due to a mess yesterday with my final chemo drugs we were told a delay would occur today as well. Thankfully, that was not the case. At 10:30 they came in and gave me medication and did the transplant. At that point I was very thankful because I was not feeling so well this morning and did not want to struggle through the day. Once I woke up from transplant meds I have been feeling much better. I have taken a walk and ordered dinner and hope to be able to enjoy it a bit. My digestive system is not cooperating at its best and anything drink taste like nothing... really gross. So, Todd got me some Gatorade that has helped some.

I have had so many thoughts and simply not sure what to write. It's hard being sick, seeing others sick, realizing this is my life today... what is life? Last night after hours of ice and walking to stay away, I simply was thankful to have survived another day. What will tomorrow hold? I have no clue. They tell me not to worry and everyone's body is different, so I'm hoping mine will be the "good body" this time and the side effects minimal. Keeping weight on and eating is a challenge and no one likes that starving feeling in your stomach that makes you feel sick, when all you want is food. So, back to one day at a time, a large part of the hard part is behind us and now, one more tough week and recovery. I am depending on God to strengthen me each step, I've no other choice. I'm trusting my nurses and doctors to care for me the best they know how and I'm reminded that compared to many rooms I've walked by lately in the hospital. I have it pretty good. Praying for complete healing and that life will soon be back to "normal" better than ever... being with my loved ones and getting to love on my family and kiddos! If, I'm feeling well tomorrow the kids will come up to visit, so pray it's a good day! Thanks... Heidi

November 18, 2014 – long overdue update

So, I am up early this morning, thinking that could be a good thing. I finally had a good night! PTL Yesterday had really rough moments, melt downs, medications... but I finally feel a bit normal this morning. I am having continual side effects. The side effects have been minimal, so thank you for all your prayers. There are just still many side effects even at a minimal situation lead from one thing to another. Continued fever - but the Dr. said I do not have to take Tylenol! The liquid I spit all over the place (gag reflex) and then they started crushing it and putting in in food that already tasted terrible. Yuck! They say the body simply responds with fever when counts are down. They have ruled out all serious infections and expect it will stop once my counts and platelets bounce back. but fever means blood draws not once but twice... and then a fever twice mean blood draws again. Constant smells, medications the whole thing seriously just makes you feel awful. I seriously can't wait to be able to really eat food again or drink water and it to taste refreshing. I mainly do Ice chips... about all I can tolerate. I do not have mouth sores, I have digest issues from the chemo drug. Liquid in causes stomach issues and stomach issues... well, they are many and I will spare you all the details. Today, I plan to start with Chicken Noodle soup and will pray my body will tolerate it, if so I will feel as though I have turned a corner. I have some pain issues that need to be resolved but the process is slow. Pray for healing to my body.

I have talked to hardly anyone, the amount of energy required for conversation has been much. Hoping today will be my turn around day, they keep telling me it is coming and then I have another bad day. Hopeful! due to my good night but I haven't tried food yet, so we shall see. Afraid of nausea, have begun to prefer vomiting but not always an option... okay, no one wanted to know that. It's just been challenging for sure. Dr. said, I probably need another week, yesterday, so I guess Monday but hoping for sooner. I will say the time has gone fast. I have had amazing nurses! I guess I'm a pretty good patient :) as well. Yesterday might have been the exception... Well, thank you all for continued prayers I need them for sure, the days have been hard. Thank you for more cards and posters for my room with Bible verses! I love them and there are A LOT of people in and out of my room on a daily basis, you have no idea... a man came in twice the other day, saying "transportation" I kept telling him, No, I had plans to go nowhere... many notice my decorations! I hear my house and yard are cared for and I am thankful for that :) Of course the kids will have a week to mess it up... just kidding, sure they would never do that :) We are continually reminded we do NOT do this alone! God has sent an army to care for us and we will never be able to repay everyone for all they have done, so Thank You! It's all we can say! I am confident that God will allow many opportunities in the future for us to minister to you and those around us, who Need Him and His love! We will do for others as they have done for us, we are truly blessed! Hoping today is a great day! Heidi

> We are continually reminded we do NOT do this alone! God has sent an army to care for us.

November 19, 2014 – update

Well, now that I feel I have somewhat come back from the dead I will try to update specifics. Yesterday, My Dr. was excited about my counts, He said they were moving up and there were some very healthy cells they don't usually see this soon that my body was already producing. When I mentioned that I felt well enough to call my kids he smiled. He said regardless of my counts the best indicator is small things like this... wanting to talk to family and feeling well enough! It shows him I am healing. He mentioned my counts would have to minimally be 1 before consideration of going home, in addition to other health issues resolving themselves. He assumed by Friday they should be 1. My nurse just said, they are 1 now!!!!!!! So, many praises on that part. I am feeling okay in many ways but there are still a few pain and digest issues.

I need prayers that my body will accept food. Yesterday, I kept breakfast :) lunch consisted of 5 bites of food... dinner 2 bites of applesauce and within 5 minutes I was randomly vomiting. Strangest thing ever... I still managed to feel well after that, at this point I prefer my body just reject the food in the moment as opposed to feeling nauseous. So, today we start over, I just ate some soup and my stomach is far from quiet, it has a lot to say. So, I wait and hope today my body will begin to accept the food it needs. I am able to drink a bit more water too, ice chips have been about it. The small things in life we take for granted. My kids made home made Peanut Butter cups with Grandma and were so excited wanting to send me some :) I will love them in a few weeks :) Everything, looks so good but then eating, well, another story. I also have a few pain issues

going on. My Dr. stated that with these issues my body will fight harder sending all my good cells there to try to repair. Some repairs need to be made before they are going to release me. So, please pray this can be gotten under control in the next few days. I can handle pain, better than ick, honestly. Just frustrating.

Tomorrow, I am hoping due to my counts the Dr. will allow our youngest to come visit. She has the day off school and has not gotten to come due to her age and restrictions. Daddy plans to then take her to the Art Museum for a few hours. So, pray that works out and that I feel well! Overall, if I'm in bed, I'm good, if I'm up and moving a little icky. Yes, ick and icky are my words :) Well, blessing to y'all today! My NA just came into my room and stopped and ohhhh and aweeeed over my Verses/Posters on the walls, she read each one and commented on how she loved them all! We continue to be surrounded by amazing workers and nurses! so thankful!... I think I'll cl with Ephesians 3:20-12 asking that God who is ABLE will continue to do more than we can ask or imagine in regards to healing this old body! To Him be the glory! If you need a good laugh, follow the link below... just for fun! Heidi[22]

November 20, 2014 – Counts have jumped!!!!!

For those not on FB I wanted to not leave you out of this big loop! My counts have jumped from 1.1 to 4.2 today!!!!! Very good! I will have to wait for rounds to hear from my Dr. and what they officially have to say but going home this weekend is looking good. My body has healed much in regards to my pain issues in the last 24 hours. I prayed please God! Heal me quickly, more quickly than I know is normal and He has done that. I just ate almost a whole hard-boiled egg, some English Muffin with PB and 1/2 piece of bacon... and my stomach is not churning! A shower is in my near future and I'm beginning to feel a bit like, ME, again :) So, keep praying I would love to go home on Saturday and I'm not opposed to asking to go home Friday night if I'm feeling really good and the Dr. are pleased with all my counts! Thankful for our Army of prayer warriors who have helped bring us through this! God has been so Faithful! Heidi

5

Recovery

With her chemo and stem cell replacement behind her, Heidi finally began the road to recovery. Since her hospitalization, we have experienced new joys and continual reminders that the Lord is faithful.

November 23, 2014 – I'm home!

So, I did not realize 'til just now after reading an e-mail that if you are not in the FB world you might not know I was home! Well, my counts jumped from the beginning of the week to the end better than expected. I was told I could go home on Saturday, and had wondered "Well, if my counts are really good, maybe I'll ask to go home on Friday." My Dr. had stated they would see me on Monday for a check-up and blood work so Saturday to Monday was about all they were willing to let me go before being "checked on," I get it. They expect to see you 2-3 times for a few weeks after transplant. So, even though it's over... it's not over. On Friday morning the Doctors came in and said my counts were great! and I could go home. I was confused, like today???? Yes. We were not really ready to go home... our bathroom was being re-done and we had family still at the house and I wasn't sure I felt completely well enough for a reunion with the kids. Sure, I missed them but they are a bit overwhelming... so, we told the Doc's we would get a hotel close to the hospital and we got a good night's rest, without being wakened every few hours before returning home. So, for those praying for a Friday release, we got it! God answered!!!!!! He has been so faithful!

Saturday we were excited to come home and see the kids. They were all home (not working) and we were able to enjoy a very cool Poster they made me, more like a banner! Some good visiting! We were thankful for family who have cared for them! I think they were a bit worn out :) We have a very busy household and much to care for, could not have done it without you. My only requirements are ever that the house be standing and all children be alive! If you have managed that, you have done a great job! I never worried once I was away! God was faithful again!

I have many spiritual things brewing in my head for another day! I will say I need prayers especially for the next 20 days! For 30 days post-transplant I have to be very careful of germs. This is difficult when you realize how many germs there really are. One of my children is sick now and that makes it really hard. You begin to realize how many things they touch. So, pray for protection over my body as it heals. I have to go to the hospital twice this week. They tell me it's the only place I need to wear a mask, gotta love it! They need me to come the worst place for germs :)

the hospital! So, again, protection! I also am very weak. I need to gain weight to gain strength. I think I will begin to get rid of the daily sick feeling if I can keep eating and get stronger. My appetite is not bad. It really took a shift the day I left the hospital. I am able to eat and most things taste well, just only able to eat a little before feeling full. So, lots of little meals. I'm ready for the sick feeling to subside! I got really sick of swallowing pills at one point simply could not do it. So, I am prone to not take a bunch of medications, just waiting for the icky to stop.

> God is doing great things always! We might have to stop and look or change our perspective! We see what we choose to see!

In addition to praying for me, as you have so faithfully, Please continue to pray for Todd. It's just been a lot. There is still much to balance as I cannot grocery shop or clean much etc. Todd will still be balancing many extra responsibilities. I am able to do a little. They do not want me in bed all day so 15 mins here or there. I am thankful to be able to think and process! I still get over stimulated easily but I can balance reading, with a nap and some catching up with friends. I am able to have visitors who are well! If you would like to come visit, I would love that. Just call or msg me. I think I might get bored, unless I start feeling much better and then I will never be bored, always much to do... even if I'm stuck at home:) For, now, I am resting... one nap a day seems to be getting me by and then early bedtime. I slept from 10:30- 6:30 last night, I couldn't believe it when I woke up! After crazy sleeping schedule and tons of medications, I was beginning to wonder how long before I would be able to sleep on my own! Only a few nights apparently! Praise God! Signing off for now but will be back. Thanksgiving is this week and I have celebrated it many days already! Tears of Joy! True Joy at all God has done in me, through me, in our family and through our family! Miracles right in front of our eyes, impossible to miss! Don't miss the good despite the bad, it's there. Maybe it's not a healing from Cancer but God is doing great things always! We might have to stop and look or change our perspective! We see what we choose to see! Choose this week to count your blessings and be thankful whether it's a time of blessing or a time of hardship... God is there with you and He is working it together for your good and His Glory! Heidi

December 2, 2014 – Post Transplant

So, today I am at about 20 days post-transplant. I am to wait 'til 30 before I'm okay to go out and of course, still be cautious of germs but at least have a bit more freedom. Being home is hard, not feeling my best, a challenge. The days go pretty fast, I have learned to be still, to think, to pray when I'm physically tired but unable to sleep. My counts are good, my days are improving. Yesterday I did not take any medications at all so, that was encouraging. I feel a bit stronger each day.

Today, I have many thoughts and words... I think Joy and Trust are at the top of my list for some deep thoughts. I felt nothing but true Joy the first day after transplant that I began to feel better. I listened to worship music all day and cried on and off. There is no way to express the feelings. When you have no idea how you will get through something and then before you know it you are on the other side... it's an amazing feeling. A realization of who God is and what He is capable of doing! Ps. 30:5b "Weeping may endure for the night, but Joy comes in the morning" I realize Joy just comes... it comes when a baby is born or someone gets married, there are many occasions. We often don't think of Joy coming after pain, suffering and sorrow, but let me tell you it does. If you Know Christ, you are able to experience that true Joy that comes from watching Him work... let alone work in your own personal life in a life changing way!

Today I read an interesting verse in Ps. 21:4 ESV *"He asked life of you, you gave it to him."* I thought, that was me... I asked of God... to give me life! To allow me to live and he granted it. What a gift, not everyone is given. Ps. 21 and 22 talk of Joy in His presence! I am thankful to have experienced such great Joy! but then I'm reminded how quickly life goes "back to normal" everyday stuff and we almost forget what God has done, we have to remind ourselves. We look at trust... trust God we say... How? we ask... we have to let go of stuff, it's so hard. I trusted God with Cancer once, and then again, it returned... was the trust still there from the first time, honestly, NO, not immediately. I had to re-trust, if that is a term... I had to remind myself God was big enough. I had to work through feelings and emotions yet again. Now, I'm through it and I look at life and how many other things I must trust God with... my life, my family, my finances... there is a daily long list of ways I must trust God. I see how easy it is to slip back to hanging on to stuff, people, relationships, it's like it's automatic with us, we are so focused on God and then life just rushes back in trying to take over.

Today, I'm reminded I have to let go of everything in life, it's God's! My husband, my children, our finances, our relationships... All His! Psalm 22:4-5 ESV *"In YOU our Fathers, trusted, they trusted and YOU delivered them. To YOU they cried and were rescued..."* God has cared for me, I have done my best to trust Him through it all... but today, I'm reminded trusting Him does not end just because Cancer, Lord willing, is gone. Trusting Him is a daily, moment by moment choice! Joy comes through that trusting, through spending that time with Him, reminding myself of who He is and What He alone can do... Well, those are my deeps thoughts for today. Friday I go back to the Dr. for a check-up and they will continue to keep an eye on me. I will have scans at 100 days so probably early February. Until then, I challenge you and myself, to trust God... one day at a time with everything! Through it all, I've learned to trust in Jesus! and will continue to, I don't believe the journey ever ends, this side of heaven! Love you all and so thankful! Heidi

December 12, 2014 – Home for 3 weeks already!

So, as I look at the calendar I realize another 3 weeks have flown by... where do the days go? I am amazed. This week on Thursday I hit 30 days post-transplant. My Dr. appointments have been really good. I have been told, I look great and am doing amazing. Ahead of schedule! All of which is a huge praise. This week has been interesting for me. I went from the beginning of the week to being really frustrated, still feeling not myself, and tiredness hitting hard at times. I could manage a little over 1 hour of activity before needing to rest and was still needing an hour or two nap each day. As the week has progressed I would get up and think... I think I feel good today. Then, I would almost wait expecting to feel sick. I am happy to tell you the sickness has begun to subside as a whole. I have small amounts of time but not all day or even half a day. I have felt more and more myself with each passing day.

> Through it all, I've learned to trust in Jesus! and will continue to, I don't believe the journey ever ends, this side of heaven!

My goal this week has been to re-train my appetite! Sounds weird but I would wake up feeling really sick, starving! like a pit was in my stomach. I would eat every hour all morning and then it was like my body would catch up... when your stomach shrinks the body plays tricks on itself. It's a small space so it fills up really fast... but even though I'm "full" my stomach will growl and demand more food but I simply cannot hold it. The mind knows I need more food but it's on a different page from my stomach. So, all that to say, it's getting better. I decided if I'm hungry all the time anyway, I will spread out my meals to where they need to be with small snacks and re-train my body to what is normal. I am feeling stronger this week. I was able to go all day without a nap yesterday, first day in 3 weeks! I did not plan to skip the nap, just forgot the kids got out of school early on Thursday so they were home and no nap occurred. I did sleep well though last night. So, much to be thankful for over the last 3 weeks!

In all honestly though the past couple weeks have been a real struggle for me. Hormones get really messed up from Chemo so you have to add that to the mix. My emotions have been all over the place. My mind wants to do stuff and my body says "I just can't" it's a really frustrating process. I find myself often in deep thought though of how cancer, although a major thing... is kinda over, dare I say now life will slowly go back to normal. I have seen many commercials, being in the hospital of those with Diabetes, or Heart disease... just lots of illnesses that have reminded me that some deal with pain, sickness and medical struggles daily. My daily, is somewhat temporary... it's hard to imagine being sick all the time, or in pain all the time or Dr. appointments all the time. For some this is a way of life, I feel like I have been given a taste of both worlds... I have so many thoughts but honestly they are not complete enough for me to share... I have daily struggles. How can I complain or be ungrateful or frustrated when God has brought me through so much, how does the human mind quickly go back to normal and almost immediately forget what God has done? Some days I'm just a mess, trying to figure it all out. I think being sick and what feels like too much time to think, can be an issue for me. Some say, I'm too hard on myself... I am working to find balance midst so much chaos for the last two years. What does God have for me now? My husband says a blog... still thinking about that one. I have moments I have much to say and other moments nothing seems clear. Life is hard... we have to choose what to focus on and yes, even me after cancer twice, I'm having trouble... sometimes life seems surreal, like it's not yours, like really? did I just go through all of that????!!!! You don't always have lots of time to process because life stops and then boom, it's back!

I know God is working in me and teaching me and I still have so much to learn. I know this... I am loved by God. I am important to Him. He has a plan for my life, even when it doesn't always feel like it. He is using all my experiences and yours to draw me closer to Him, to make me more like Him. He is allowing all this so if I will allow it... to bring glory back to Him. Some days it's so clear and others I have lots of questions. I know I am not alone in this journey of trying to understand and accept life. For today, I will choose to live the life God has given me... I always feel like I should be doing more... our lives should impact others, our light for Christ should shine for Him... honestly, I write here and enjoy it, it gives me an outlet. I feel I am like Moses, saying "God, I need an Aaron" feel I need someone to speak for me when it comes to speaking face to face, I am really bad with words and conversations... my mind often feels blank. I think that is why I think so much, always trying to figure out how to speak, what to say... but still feel bad at it. Here, I am able to think and process with no unknown factor of what will the "other person" say and how will I respond. I am free to share and you will like it or not like it :) I can clearly, sometimes, express my thoughts not knowing what those who read it think... Well, I feel now as if I am rambling... life is just hard and full of struggles even when we have so much to thank and praise God for... this week I'm going to intentionally try to focus more on the good of life! It's life, it's a gift! We are never guaranteed tomorrow... thankful for today! God says... Do not

> Our lives should impact others, our light for Christ should shine for Him.

worry about tomorrow... well, that is hard :) Today, I will do my best... This is the day the Lord has made I will rejoice and be glad in it! Today... I will live today! Heidi

January 10, 2015 – 2 months ago today!

On November 10th I had my transplant, today is January 10th and I can hardly believe 2 months have gone by. Just a short update, well we will see if it's actually short :) I will see my Dr. on Jan 23rd and from there 100-day scans will be scheduled. I have had all good reports from blood work. Holidays were good for us. I was very thankful that I had planned ahead and had all my shopping done and gifts wrapped. I would have never been able to do it. As for how I feel today... well, I cannot complain! I have no pain or sickness, thank God. I am able to do all daily chores that are necessary. You quickly learn what has to be done and what does not have to be done. So, I can do all the basics, small grocery trips for necessities, dinner on the table each night, and back to carpooling kids. God has been good. I still get tired easily. I am able to go several days without naps and then it catches up with me and I need some extra sleep. Not a big deal though.

He has a plan even when I don't understand it, even when it's hard and it hurts.

We were thankful to see and spend time with extended family for the Holidays. I was a bit nervous of sickness. I am happy to say we have been "sick free" despite many around us being sick. Our youngest even shared a bed with her cousin, while we were home and her cousin had strep just a day later and she did not get sick. Just thankful for God's protection over our family and myself. Although I have been feeling much better I honestly still need much prayer. Some days I simply don't feel myself. Just struggle because I cannot do all I want to, often emotions are there and I realize I'm just weak still and tired. Holidays helped me gain my weight back making me physically stronger. I have started a few exercises as well but it's all a slow process. Learning to be patient is hard.

I've said before and will say again, Hard is hard, whether it's cancer or just day to day life. I get so frustrated at bad days thinking, "Heidi, you did cancer, why can't you handle this little thing?" Well, I'm not sure... I can handle it, it's just hard, over and over again. Life is about so much, so much thinking and learning and teaching... I just get tired. I keep reminding myself, it's only been 8 weeks. I simply cannot handle the stresses of life as I once could, but God knows that and is so patient with me, as well as my family. I'm very happy to report that last week while home seeing family we went Ice Skating at Notre Dame... for almost 2 hours I skated and then almost 3 hours I slept, LOL... it felt amazing to be on the ice, free, feeling well, a reminder of the healing that God has brought in my life!!!! The next day we had a bowling party and I was able to bowl as well, hand sanitizer after touching anything! Again, thankful to be able to do some fun things with my family. Reminded of the gift of health!

My news for the last week is my head has sprouted!!!! Yes, my hair is growing back! The top of my head is fuzzy and feels like velvet and if you get close enough (my hair is all very light blonde) my eye brows have sprouted as well. When new hair comes in it sticks straight out until it gets long enough to lay down... I complained a bit a few weeks ago because I felt like I had a rash on my stomach and back, bumps everywhere... a few nights ago I started laughing while laying in bed, the bumps? Hair follicles opening for the new hair to grow back... OH! I had forgotten this happened last time after chemo and hair loss. How quickly we forget things. I was showing the kids the hair on my fingers even standing up and one said, we have hair on our fingers? Believe it or not you don't really miss most of your hair, just the hair on your head :) So, hair growth indicates healing is taking place and although slow, it has begun, this week even...

> He speaks of Joy, but that Joy comes from HIM, not our circumstances.

Well, my husband still says I need to start a blog, I feel I blog all the time just in my head, so many thoughts and so hard to get them all in the right order to put them down on paper. I am often saying the wrong words in sentences and then laugh, part of chemo... the brain does its own thing sometimes. I am thankful for the speed in which God has chosen to heal me. I will ask for continued prayers for upcoming scans, my rational mind says they will be good but the emotional mind says," it's not possible for them to be bad, is it?" Life is full of fears and uncertainties. I cried last week as I heard my friend's 4-year-old had been diagnosed with cancer. I simply cannot understand the ways of God, I can't! But I am reminded that the devil is always there, trying to work and plant seeds of doubt. I am confident that God loves me and You! He gave up His own life for me and you! He has a plan even when I don't understand it, even when it's hard and it hurts. We have much uncertainty in our lives right now... fear and uncertainty are not just part of cancer, they are part of life. In this life God promised, there will be trouble, but do not be afraid I have overcome the world. God never promised it would be easy, He promised us Him and with Him, heaven after this life. He speaks of Joy, but that Joy comes from HIM, not our circumstances... hard to swallow... Blessings to you all this 2015! You have been faithful prayers partners and we are so grateful.

January 28, 2015 – Flying by...

The weeks keep flying by, seems I just updated but it's been a few weeks. I saw the Dr. last Friday and all is well. He said my counts are good. I saw a nurse and she said I looked great for 2 months after transplant. I told her I'm not sure what you are supposed to feel like but others seem to think I'm doing great and I can't complain. God has been so faithful. He continues to work in my heart about life. I'm so thankful for each day. I am happy to report that I have always had stomach issues and the chemo from the transplant has seemed to have "fixed" the problems, my stomach has been great! A blessing from the trial. I find that daily life is still much slower for me. I get all I need to get done but life just feels like it's in slow motion still sometimes. If I'm talking to you and you wonder if I'm taking it all in... probably not :) My processing life seems slower too, but I think the Dr. indicated it will get better with time. We live in such a busy, fast paced world. I have begun to really enjoy days like today where I don't have to go anywhere. I can take time listening and worshiping God. I made soup and I just took a walk. I have been feeling like exercising so I bundled up and off I went. It was refreshing. Todd and I also got a small retreat in Chicago this weekend, since we had to go for my Dr. appointment. We did nothing exciting, except my eating a whole piece of Cheesecake from the Cheesecake factory, that was pretty exciting! We just enjoyed the time together and we were thankful to have it, after such a crazy 2014. We pray for rest this year... pressing on, Trusting God each step of the way. We have many big things happening this year already but confident God is in control and He does not need me to fret and worry... He can handle it. He does not need me at all, But Praise God, He chooses to use me... so thankful. My PET and CT scans are tentatively set for February 19th, waiting on Insurance approval. Confident they will be good! Always believing God has His best in store for us! Thank you all for your continued prayers... Heidi

February 20, 2015 – 100 day scans

Hello, friends and family. Yesterday I had my 100 day scans, my scans ran right up until the time to see the Dr. so we were going off quickly read scans, preliminary reads from the Radiologist. The reading said, no suspicious activity! Today I got confirmation from the finals readings! Praise God! I am really processing this information at a slow pace. Not sure how to explain that. I know last time they said, remission and I never looked back so this time it's hard to just accept it. I am, don't get me wrong but I think my body and mind need to get caught up.

Well, I just hit a button and my two paragraphs disappeared, maybe God didn't want me to say all that... I will say this, I wanted to hear the Dr. say you are cancer free, when I asked, "Is the cancer gone?" he responded with "there is no scan that tells if the cancer is gone" The scans simply indicate if there is activity in the nodes that should not be there and they look for things to be symmetrical. Mine are reading no suspicious activity! He did also say he would see me in three months, even though his other patients are still coming every month :) another indication of the true healing that God has brought about in my body. My counts were all very good! Repeat CT's in 6 months. Allowing us to enjoy Spring and Summer!

It always takes me days to process life and cancer but I wanted to let y'all know our news and thank you for continued prayers. All I know is God has taught me to slow down. Some by choice and some because cancer twice, naturally slows you down. I have learned, as I'm not sure I did the first time, to enjoy now, today, each moment. I feel like I am simply sitting and absorbing life itself. Each moment with those I love. Cancer is part of my past, part of my story and reality is it could someday again be part of my future. I pray this not true and I will choose to not live in fear of the big C word... but I will choose to live, to be thankful that God has given me life each day and it is a gift, you are a gift... each breath a gift. We are excited about 2015, God is doing much in our lives and our family. Todd said on Sunday, the only thing is life that is certain is change... our lives continue to change but I'm thankful for a God who goes before us and leads the way. Praying for the many changes that 2015 is bringing in our lives. Thankful to be a part of them... but tired! Thankful for you all and the role you have played in our lives over these two years! God has truly blessed us! Enjoy each day! Heidi

February 24, 2015 – It's long... Life after crisis

So, there is this story in the book of Acts that I read this week. The story goes back to a song I sang as a child.

> Peter and John went to pray, they saw a lame man by the way. He held out his palms and said give me some alms and this is what Peter did say... Silver and Gold have I none but such as I have, give I thee (love the KJV) in the name of Jesus Christ of Nazareth, rise up and walk! He went... walking and leaping and praising God, walking and leaping and praising God.

I have been struggling for days and simply couldn't find a way to figure it out, why the struggle, and how to articulate the struggle. I decided today that this struggle is not just about me and cancer but I feel many feel similar things after a crisis. What is crisis? It's different for all, I don't have an exact definition. I will let you decide for yourself... if you relate, then likely you have experienced some sort of crisis in your own life.

All that to say, I have praised God for healing! But I don't feel much like my emotions and response have been appropriate... I feel like I should be radiating Joy, I should be leaping and praising God, there should be this great response to my Dr. telling me, Heidi, your scans are clean. I guess some of my immediate response was, are you sure? Will you change your mind when the final report comes in? How long will it last? Doubt! Yes, that's it. Natural in some ways I believe. I think of Doubting Thomas, I want to see and feel for myself. I too, want to know for sure... Before I will believe. Christ's death and resurrection was for sure, it was true. Praise God!!!! In this life, though, a clean scan can be temporary, unfortunately. My body appears healthy now and I feel mostly healthy but my mind is not the same... my ability to think, process, plan, handle stress... it is weak. I am tired. I think it's easy to treat those in these situations like, it's over and now all should be back to normal. Crisis changes, everyday life.

> I will choose to live, to be thankful that God has given me life each day and it is a gift, you are a gift... each breath a gift.

Crisis changes you. It has changed me. I can't explain it really but today a thought came to me. I'm a survivor... I think that's it! In order to survive, I have had to sit my emotions on the side, to some degree and just handle what is in front of me. There is no choice in crisis. Like it or not, the path was chosen for you and you must survive. So, you figure out how to do that... survivors are strong. They endure – hard things. When Crisis hits it's like we are programed to "learn how to survive" ... The problem is that those loving and supporting are celebrating at healing and you are left to say... I survived, now what? Why do I not feel excited? How do you change your thinking back from "I must survive today" to "it's over!!!" Go back to living, when everything has been far from normal for so long, unpredictable, hard?... Many days of no stimuli... simply lying in a bed waiting for that day to end, hoping the next would be better! I would think it would be easier to just put it behind and move forward, it's not! I'm finding it a process of re-learning. People are no longer taking care of me, I'm well. Now we are back to me taking care of everyone, again. Huh? How quickly life changes... sometimes not leaving us enough time to catch our breath and adjust.

> Crisis changes you. It has changed me.

I remember my day of praising God clearly, my day of Joy and tears, it was over 3 months ago. For me, it was the day in the hospital when I went from my worst day physically to my turn around day... I felt physical healing, I knew better days were to come, I knew God had carried me through the valley, a long dark valley some days.

You go from quiet, I rarely watched TV or talked to anyone, reading was also not much of an option. Just surviving moment by moment. I simply was in tune with God, talking to Him, reading my verses posted on my wall in my room, hour after hour. I am kinda stuck there... I now love to just sit, think or sometimes, think nothing. I'm okay with lying in the chair under an electric blanket and reading all day and if nothing else gets done, well, does it matter? I want to be with people, feel connected but then in the same moment I don't. I'm tired, I want to rest, talking is so much for my brain to process most days. I enjoy the silence. I feel confused by the battle within.

Today I experienced my struggle. A simple day really. I exchanged cars with my daughter to get her an oil change. I planned to come to the High school and exchange cars back after all done. I knew what lot she was to park in. So, I drove over to the school. I drove up and down the 4-5 isles looking for my truck. I saw a truck that looked like mine but I immediately thought... "no, it's shiny and new" You see, my truck is covered in salt. Last time I washed it, the next day it looked exactly the same. So, I was looking for a dirty blue Expedition. I even looked at the back of the only truck I saw that looked like mine and it said it was an Expedition but again, really didn't look like mine. So, I drove in front of it and then I realized, definitely NOT mine, it has a tag hanging from the rearview mirror and mine does not have that, So, I continued to be confused as to where my truck was... spending probably 15 minutes looking. In a moment of almost giving up, I decided, maybe that is my truck. Then slowly my brain starts piecing things together. I remember that Todd drove my truck last night and I think "maybe he washed it" I begin to think, maybe Ashley grabbed her tag and put it in my truck so she didn't get into trouble at school. So, I drive over and park. Even sitting next to it, I still was not convinced it was my truck, but yes! it was... I got out and looked in and there was my stuff. This story sounds pretty normal, maybe, LOL... or you are thinking – "Heidi, your hair was blonde" ... but instead of laughing I found myself crying. Not really upset, just a realization that my brain is not healed, my life is not back to normal. Not sure what normal is supposed to be... I would have figured this out really fast before. I was great at handling lots of stress and details and now it's like, my brain won't work right.

Two years of Cancer and treatments has left me – Alive! Praise God! God has given me another chance at life. He has work for me to do but I have no clue what that is at this time, other than loving my husband and children! I think that alone is a pretty high calling. Our life continues to be full of transitions, major stuff that many would fall apart just trying to handle one thing, yet our plate is always full. This is a God thing! His strength, His timing... His way! This year, I know that God will take my thinking from Survivor thinking to being healed and back to being able to figure out, how to live this thing called – Life. Life is a gift, I think we make it so much more than God ever intended it to be. We make it about stuff, busyness, projects... He just wants time with us and we need to just enjoy that time with God and the time He has given us with those we love. Each day, a gift... I feel like I'm just trying to soak in life... all this cold weather is making it hard! I want to walk outside, see kids playing and laughing, I want to soak in the warmth of life. I want to cherish relationships that God has given me and not ever take them for granted, thinking I have tomorrow because cancer or no cancer I'm still not guaranteed tomorrow.

So, life will continue to be slow for me, for a time. First year I had cancer I bounced back to normal life no problem, I see this past year resulting differently. Slower, more physical and mental healing that needs to take place. A time of rest ahead... still dependent on my ever faithful husband. I feel myself holding back from things I would have once just done... wondering can I do all this, should I put this on the calendar, how tired will I get if I choose to do this... do I need to save my energy to be the best I can for my family and for caring for them? Thoughts I never, ever thought would come. Some days, I have to choose and I don't like that but God never promised life would be easy, only that we will not walk it alone! So, by my side, He is! He has been and will forever be! Faithful in crisis and out... This will be a year of learning how to live again, how to not hold back, how to let go and another year of change for our family! I think I'm used to change, not sure I like it still but used to it. Learning always to rest in God and where He has me. Working hard to communicate what is really going on in my life and heart and mind... even when I don't like it. Praying that God will direct me in what is next in this journey called life... Love God, Love others... Share God with others... Pray for others... Continually thankful for all of you and your prayers! Please continue! With much praise and thanks! Heidi

March 6, 2015 – Thoughts

So, this week I read a book... I am a very slow reader and was surprised how quickly I got through this book in particular. A book Todd read while I was in the hospital getting my transplant, at the time reading was not something I could really do. So, this was the week God wanted me to read it, the week I was ready to hear and relate and connect. The book is called *The Hardest Peace* by Kara Tippetts.[23] Todd and I were talking about Kara as if we knew her from reading the book and her blog. Our daughter said, who is Kara? Oh, just a person in a book... but not just any person. Kara is a young woman writing as she is dying of cancer. Her journey is almost over... she got to live to see her book published but she is at the end of her journey. As I read I related to so many things some of which I would like to share with you and encourage you to think about your life.

Kara and her husband have had to focus on heaven. They have had to teach their kids what they REALLY believe and live it out in front of them. They have had to be honest that Mommy won't be here for your "next big thing." She mentions how we often live for the next big thing, event, date, project, vacation... whatever you are living for next when she has come to realize... "I won't likely be here for their next big thing." She mentions she has had to cherish each moment, cherish the small things not just the next big thing. The hugs, kisses, the smiles, the laughter, the snuggles when you are too sick to even move. I have begun to live this way. It did not happen after my first battle with cancer, I quickly found myself back in the craziness of life again. This time is different though. I wonder if it's possible to get here, without crisis... can one just realize how precious life is?[24]

"Cancer has given me the freedom to see my story with me utterly not in it... I saw the grace of care and community when I could not reciprocate my love to the givers. Cancer showed me the beautiful community that could be built into a church that didn't have me doing anything. Cancer showed me the gift and strength of weakness, that in the place of utter inability, Jesus was able." Kara[25]

She pointed out it's like she is watching from a distance. She is seeing life, without her in it. She used to think things won't get done, if I don't do them. Sickness has showed her that things will get done, differently, but they get done. Church goes on, school goes on, jobs continue and life with kids in the house never stops... but often she is just watching... realizing as we should, someday we will be gone and life will go on without us. She says, "the messy of our life happened before, but our self-conscious noticing stopped. Our jam-stained counters and endless piles of life in corners simply went unnoticed... life mattered more than tidy living"[26]

I am reminded that God does not need me, really, He does not. He loves me and has a plan for me, but He does not need me to do, all the things I think I must do or "life, will fall apart" No, it won't. God teaches us and molds us in those quiet moments but often we have no time for quiet moments. Something to think about.

***She speaks "Cancer is a gift. There, I said it. I can say that cancer and suffering give the beautiful gift of perspective. It is the gift you never wanted, the gift wrapped in confusion and brokenness and heartbreak. It's the gift that strips all your other ideas of living from you completely. The beautiful, ugly raising to the surface of the importance of each and every moment."[27] Do you even process the moments? I know I never did and now I linger in my thoughts and moments, now. I keep telling my youngest. I am just absorbing her cuteness :) She giggles... trying to enjoy each moment. In Kara's moments she sees the gift of time, she is suffering but trying to absorb each moment she is given, trusting and teaching that God's Grace is sufficient for all the moments.

... Many tidbits of what Kara says in her book... "The story that baldness brings is that everyone has entry into your illness without sharing it."[28] "In the absence of comforts and friends, is Jesus enough?"[29] "If God has called me to this hard story, His promise is one of sufficient grace. Sufficient for me, sufficient for my guy, sufficient for my littles."[30]

"Trusting God when the miracle does not come, when the urgent prayer gets no answer, when there is only darkness - this is the kind of faith God values perhaps most of all" ... Nancy Guthrie, Holding on to Hope[31]

She is so real in her book. I love this about her. She speaks not of fear of dying or of what Heaven will be, she knows her place is with God. She is very honest though about imagining life without herself. Imagining all the moments she will miss and how her children and husband will go on without her. She is honest about not wanting to go... we are to long for heaven but it's so easy to want what this earth has to offer, don't get me wrong, God desires good things for us here :) I often struggled with these same thoughts... Yeah, God, I know heaven is going to be great and I can't imagine it but I really want to stay... Thankful for each day!

A friend spoke to Kara... "Dear heart, the purpose of life is not longevity." She shared how she both loved and hated the words. Westminster Confession asks this "What is the chief end of man?" ... to Glorify God and enjoy him forever... in this life and the next. We dream of tomorrow and growing old with those we love but God never promised that... We are to glorify Him in the story He has given us, to be faithful in the Hard, to have Peace in the suffering...

All these thoughts are mine from Kara's Book, I will post the link. Her perspective on life is one not written and spoken often... I encourage you to read it. To embrace each day, each moment, even the hard ones... A favorite song has lyrics... "Every day when you wake up breathing, every night when you close your eyes, every day that your heart keeps beating... there's purpose for your life!" Ashes Remain[32]... Don't let today just come and go full of busyness take time to realize God has a purpose for you, even as Kara is counting down her final days as I write this[33]... there's purpose for her life, each breath! She has been faithful to tell her story. We all have a story to tell... You are here, for a Reason! Love you all... thanks for listening. Enjoy the links[34] - Heidi

July 7, 2015 – Reflections...

Hello, friends and family... it's been awhile. Summer has come and it is going fast. We have had many things on our calendar as I know you have also. I got to thinking a few weeks ago. We had some friends over and for some reason Todd pulled out some pictures from when I was in the hospital for transplant. I was kinda surprised, myself, to see them. It was really me, sick and bald. Seemed so long ago. When I realize it's only been 8 months this week, I am shocked. Seems so long ago. When I realize the amount of healing God has brought to my body, it's truly amazing. A miracle. I see myself as a walking miracle. Our friend said, I never saw these pictures... we read your posts and saw good pictures but not these. I guess back then I was in a more vulnerable state, not able to feel comfortable sharing those pictures because at the time it was so real. I will attach the pictures, if I can figure it out at the end :)[35]

As for an update, my last check-up was very good. When I shared I was often frustrated by some limitations my Doctor reminded me that I had been through much. He said it was similar to Post-Traumatic Stress Disorder. My body and mind had been placed under much stress and after I should not just expect it will act and respond the same way. I do not handle stress, or many details well. I have constant post it notes and occasionally think I've paid a bill and discover somehow I didn't. Minor things in the big scheme of life. I have more limits than I would still like, I nap often still and feel overwhelmed at life much. I have to constantly choose what to do and what not to do. In my "past" life it would have all gotten done but reality is different now and I have to let things go. God is at work in me and all around me and that is more important than all the stuff I want to accomplish. Life will likely forever be disorganized at some level. Just trying to enjoy my God, and my family each day! Thankful for each moment and all the relationships God has blessed me with.

On Sunday I will celebrate a B-day! How funny we are, not wanting to get old. Now I celebrate the privilege of getting old! a blessing... Thankful for another year.

I am doing a Bible study on Waiting... I am really enjoying just simply reading things I need to be reminded of. We spend so much time in life waiting. It's okay... God works in those times, He uses us and others in those times, He changes us in those times. We? usually hate the process :) We can't wait to grow up, to finish school, to date, to drive, to marry, to have kids to... you name it, always waiting for something. I am trying to just enjoy each moment and realize all God has taught me... in the wait. David waited years before he became King. Joseph waited years before he was over the land. He struggled through being sold, and being in jail... it was a long wait. Jesus waited and lived on this earth for 33 years... waiting for the cross. I think in His situation the wait would have been welcome. I wait for doctor's visits, now. I wait for tests and results... waiting to know what the future holds. So, as I wait... I choose to live today. Not complain, not be frustrated but patiently wait on My God! He has a plan for me. I am at a place in life I am asking Him, what is your plan for me now? The simple answer, to live today, to love my husband and my children and teach them about God and to love others. That is what you will hopefully find me doing. I know He has more in store though for the future. I will choose to wait on Him, wait on His plan... breathe truth and life into others.

I really enjoy writing here. Todd tells me I should blog but I am not full of many thoughts often. So, I have not chosen to do that at this time. I really only feel able to articulate my thoughts and feelings in writing. I often struggle and feel like Moses when he says, I need Aaron to speak for me... I feel I stumble over words when face to face and after wards, I think... I should have said this or that... always a frustration. But I know My God is BIG and has a great plan. He will use me as He sees fit. I love and enjoy people, in small doses :) I get so overwhelmed by large groups or too many people talking at once. But again, God knows all these things. I am thankful for each and every one of you and all you have meant to our family. So, I wanted to share my pictures with you now. Pictures that are a living testimony of all God has done and continues to do. The journey of Cancer and the journey of my transplant was so much... when I sit here and remember the tough days, I realize, yeah, others probably didn't realize how tough they were but that's okay... I got through them one by one with God carrying me and Todd by my side. I was so sic, I have a mental picture. I'm thankful for the pictures Todd did take so we have the memories of all the healing God has done! Truly a miracle! It's been a rough year as I have watched most of my children grieve the loss of friends they have loved, such young lives lost... we have been surrounded by much loss and grief reminding me and all of us daily that life is a gift... one to be treasured! Love you all... Heidi

Epilogue

Closing thoughts from Todd

I am writing these words one year after Heidi's stem cell replacement. She is now a year cancer free and for that we praise the Lord. Heidi continues to have struggles with recovery and especially the "chemo brain" effect of multiple rounds of poison being injected into her body. Cancer, even when treatable and curable, can be brutal on the body and has been very taxing on Heidi and the family. As you've read Heidi's thoughts through the last couple years you can see how she and I needed strength for the journey and how the Lord provided it.

To be honest, Cancer has been just one piece of our journey together. There have been other trials before and there are sure to be more to come. Yet, cancer has been unique and this has been an especially intense time for us to learn through experience what we already believed – that our God is faithful! We are thankful for His provision, for His church, for his presence and peace, for the joy we find in Him! As we continue on our journey, whatever God has in store for us, we will continue to look to Him, our rock and our redeemer.

– Todd

I have been young, and now am old,
yet I have not seen the righteous forsaken
Psalm 37:25

Appendix A

What to Remember When You Need to Remember

When crisis comes, God calls us to trust him. When circumstances are overwhelming and too much for us, that is the very time that God calls us to faith in him. In the book of Exodus, we see the nation of Israel and how they responded to their wilderness experience. When they faced the crisis of a shortage of food and water, God expected them to trust him. Instead, in their lack of faith, they longed to return to Egypt and the slavery they had endured there. They had forgotten who God was, what he promised, and how he had miraculously delivered them. We look back and think how foolish they were, in light of all they knew and had experienced, not to trust God to meet their need.

But what about us? How will *we* respond in the midst of crisis? Will our faith falter, or will we remember what we need to remember? Allow me to remind you of a few things the Israelites should have remembered and we must remember today.

First, we must remember the character of God. If we know who God is and what he is like, that should motivate us to trust him. When trouble comes, will we remember who God is? Will we remember that God is almighty? That he is sovereign? That he is in control of our circumstance? That he is good? That he is deliverer? When our circumstances seem overwhelming and too much for us we have a basis for our trust in God – his character. In the midst of a trial, we find out if we really believe about God what we say we believe. It's at these moments we need to *remember* who God is so that we will trust the Lord.

Second, we must remember the promises of God. The Bible is full of promises God has made to his people. The same God that promised deliverance from bondage for Israel promises deliverance to *us* from the bondage of sin and its consequences through the gospel. We are promised that whosoever believes in him shall not perish but have eternal life. As God's people, the Lord promises He will never leave us or forsake us. We have continued promises: that God is at work in our life to make us like Christ, that He will return, that we will spend eternity with Him in glory. And, yes, Rom 8:28 is a promise – that "all things work together for good for those who love God ..." We know to what extent we believe God's promises when we're in the midst of a crisis. We must *choose* whether or not to trust. God is indeed trustworthy. It's at these moments we need to *remember* the promises of God and trust the Lord.

Finally, we must remember the record of God. Part of our faith journey is to remember what God has done for us so that we trust in what God *will* do. We know what God has done both from what we read in Scripture and how we know Him in relationship. In both cases, remembering what God has done in the past gives us confidence as we face the future. In one of my favorite hymns, we sing "Tis so sweet to trust in Jesus, how I've proved him o'er and o'er ... Oh for Grace to trust Him more." God has shown himself to us time and time again. He has demonstrated his faithfulness to us through his word and our past experience with him. When we face a difficult circumstance, it's at these moments we need to *remember* the record of God and trust the Lord.

God is calling us to trust him We have some big hurdles in front of us, but God is able, he is Good and he is for us. Let us remember what we know of God and trust him as we glorify God and make his son known throughout the world to this generation.

Blessings,

Pastor Todd

This article appeared in our church newsletter and was based on a sermon from Exodus 15.

Appendix B

How to (and how NOT to) Minister to Families Battling Cancer

Reflecting on our past and present experience with cancer, we have been blessed to have family, friends and a church family who have been wonderfully supportive. Quite often, people want to know how they can help and encourage someone going through the experience of cancer or other medical related trials. I hope that you will find this list useful as you minister to others. Here are a few things I found to be helpful and not so helpful in our journey:

Helpful: Encouraging me to trust God through our trial

More Helpful: Sharing your experience of God's grace in your time of need and the assurance that God will be with me as well

Not Helpful: Telling me about all the people you know who also have/had cancer

Definitely Avoid: Telling me about the people you know who died from cancer

*****

Helpful: Assuring me that our doctor/hospital is a good one

More Helpful: Sharing things you found helpful during your own experience with cancer

Not Helpful: Telling me all the problems you had with my doctor or hospital

Definitely Avoid: Giving me unsolicited medical advice about alternative doctors, hospitals, or treatments

*****

Helpful: Letting me know that you are praying for me (and telling me this more than once)

More Helpful: Taking time to pray WITH me

Not Helpful: Avoiding sharing your own prayer needs so that I can be praying for you

Definitely Avoid: When I ask you to pray, telling me about someone I don't know whose problems are "worse" than mine

*****

Helpful: Sharing scriptures about the Lord's goodness and putting trust in Him

More Helpful: Sharing a passage of Scripture that was particularly meaningful to you when you were facing a similar trial

Not Helpful: Quoting Romans 8:28

Definitely Avoid: Trite (unbiblical) statements like "God doesn't give us more than we can handle"

*****

Helpful: Noticing I am discouraged and giving me a hug

More Helpful: Being there with me during the times I feel alone

Not Helpful: Not being patient with me as I struggle with my feelings and emotions

Definitely Avoid: Criticizing my emotional reaction or labelling my pain and grief as a lack of faith

*****

Helpful: Offering a shoulder if I need one

More Helpful: Taking me to coffee or lunch and then letting me share my feelings out loud

Not Helpful: Telling me you know how I feel or how you would feel if you were me

Definitely Avoid: Telling me how I SHOULD feel

*****

Helpful: Asking how we are doing or how certain things went

More Helpful: Letting me know you were thinking about/praying for us during a procedure, test, meeting, or particularly hard day

Not Helpful: Pestering me for details about things I'd like to keep private for now

Definitely Avoid: Taking it personally if I don't share all the information you want to know

*****

Helpful: Offering a specific kind of help that you can provide and you think would be helpful

More Helpful: Offering to help at a specific time or day when we will need it (like days we go to the doctor or hospital)

Not Helpful: A general "anything you need" offer

Definitely Avoid: Being upset if we don't need your help or insisting to help with things we really don't need

*****

Helpful: Offering to keep my children or help with transportation if needed

More Helpful: Taking my kids with your kids to do something fun

Not Helpful: Treating my children's concerns and feelings as trivial or unimportant

Definitely Avoid: Criticizing my kids (or my parenting)

*****

Helpful: Emails, texts, guestbook entries on our online journal, or comments on my Facebook page

More Helpful: Cards, personal notes, (short) phone calls

Not Helpful: Posting links about cancer on my FB page

Definitely Avoid: Posting personal information I shared in confidence on your prayer list or social networking site without my permission

*****

Helpful: Expressions of care and concern

More Helpful: Acts of care and concern

Not Helpful: Saying something stupid

Definitely Avoid: Avoiding me altogether because you don't know what to say (or are afraid of saying something stupid)

These are just a few thoughts from my personal experience. The main thing to realize is that families that are going through a trial need the love and support of fellow believers. God can use you to encourage, strengthen, assist, and minister to those who are battling cancer. I pray that God will use you as you reach out to others during their time of need.

This article was written by Todd and first appeared at sbcvoices.com

Appendix C

Resources for the Journey

CaringBridge

CaringBridge is a charitable 501(c)(3) nonprofit organization established in 1997 that offers free, personalized websites to people facing various medical conditions, hospitalization, medical treatment, and/or recovery from a significant accident, illness, injury, or procedure. The book you hold in your hand first appeared as journal entries on Heidi's CaringBridge site.

We knew of CaringBridge though others' journeys with cancer and found it to be a tremendously helpful way to keep people informed about Heidi's condition and allow others to journey with us.

www.caringbridge.org

Choose Hope

This company offers online sales of cancer awareness products as well as donating money back for cancer research on a monthly basis. They offer gift items and apparel for general cancer support as well as for specific types of cancer. Todd bought Hodgkin's' awareness t-shirts that he wore almost daily and to every appointment, chemotherapy session, and hospitalization.

http://www.choosehope.com/

Phil's Friends

Phil's Friends is a Christian nonprofit organization founded by two-time cancer survivor Phil Zielke. Their goal is to bring support and hope to those affected by cancer in the United States. We reach out through care packages, weekly cards, and prayer.

I was introduced to this ministry when a volunteer prayed with Max and Todd at a Christian Rap concert in Chicago. Heidi received multiple care packages and notes from this ministry throughout her cancer journey.

www.philsfriends.org

The Hardest Peace / Mundane Faithfulness Blog

Todd was first introduced through the blog and following the writings of Kara Tippetts in her battle with terminal cancer. When her book was published, Todd downloaded it on kindle and read it in a few days. Heidi later read a hard copy of the book and quotes extensively from it in her journal.

Kara eventually lost her battle with cancer, but touched many lives along the way with her raw and candid wrestling with her own feelings and her tenacious faith in the Lord and his providence. We highly recommend this book for any Christian, but especially those who may be facing hard trials like cancer.

www.mundanefaithfulness.com
www.mundanefaithfulness.com/book

Endnotes

[1] www.caringbridge.org; see Appendix C

[2] Sarah Young, *Jesus Calling: Enjoying Peace in His Presence* (Nashville: Integrity Publishers, 2004), 106.

[3] Ibid., 126.

[4] Heidi volunteers at the Women's Center of Northwest Indiana. The mission of The Women's Center ministers to women who are pregnant or considering an abortion. Their goal is to show the love of Christ in our communities by being salt and light to those making hard decisions about the life of their unborn child. www.friendsofthewc.org

[5] Jason Walker, Mark Stuart, and Nick Departee, "Carry me to the Cross," © Dayspring Music, LLC (a div. of Word Music Group, Inc.); Sweet Pacific Music (Admin. by Capitol CMG Publishing); Thirsty Moon River Publishing (Admin. by Capitol CMG Publishing); Integrity's Praise! Music (Admin. by Capitol CMG Publishing (IMI))

[6] Reuben Morgan, "Still," © 2002 Hillsong Music Publishing (Admin. by Capitol CMG Publishing)

[7] Chris Tomlin, Jason Ingram, Jonas Myrin, Martin Chalk, Matt Redman, "Sovereign" © 2012 Atlas Mountain Songs (Admin. by Capitol CMG Publishing); S. D. G. Publishing (Admin. by Capitol CMG Publishing); Said And Done Music (Admin. by Capitol CMG Publishing); sixsteps Music (Admin. by Capitol CMG Publishing); Sixsteps Songs (Admin. by Capitol CMG Publishing); Thankyou Music (Admin. by Capitol CMG Publishing); Worship Together Music (Admin. by Capitol CMG Publishing); worshiptogether.com songs (Admin. by Capitol CMG Publishing); Open Hands Music (Admin. by Essential Music Publishing LLC); Sony/ATV Timber Publishing (Admin. by Sony/ATV Music Publishing); Martin Chalk.

[8] Chris Tomlin, "Sovereign," http://www.youtube.com/watch?v=BNFmy6VHIKk

[9] When we first got married, "Footprints" was one of Heidi's favorite poems. We have a print of the poem in our living room. Our journey with cancer gives new meaning to the words.

[10] See Appendix B

[11] Beth Moore, *Living Beyond Yourself: Exploring the Fruit of the Spirit* (Nashville: LifeWay Press, 2004), 178.

[12] Ibid., 179.

[13] Ibid., 181.

[14] Amanda Cook, "You Make Me Brave," © 2013 Bethel Music Publishing

[15] W. Phillip Keller, *A Shepherd Looks at Psalm 23* (Grand Rapids, Mich: Zondervan, 2008), 38.

[16] Ibld., p. 74.

[17] Heidi posted the following videos at the end of this post:
Chris Tomlin, "Whom Shall I Fear" – https://youtu.be/cVyqmb189AE
Matt Redman, "You Never Let Go" – https://youtu.be/NM14VZVu0og

[18]Danny Gokey, "Hope in Front of Me" – https://youtu.be/9KIhYZQ_ovw

[19] Katie Davis, *Kisses from Katie: A Story of Relentless Love and Redemption* (New York: Howard Books, 2011), 136.

[20] No One Fights Alone! Is a registered trademark of Choose Hope. Choose hope is a company that sells cancer support clothing and gift items and whose profits help to support cancer research. http://www.choosehope.com

[21] Brittany Maynard took her own life on Nov 1, 2014. Kara Tippetts, herself facing terminal cancer, wrote an open letter to Brittany in which she gave a strong witness for Christ and for the sanctity of human life. See, Kara Tippetts, "Dear Brittany: Why We Don't Have to Be So Afraid of Dying & Suffering that We Choose Suicide," A Holy Experience Blog, http://bit.ly/1iMduMU

[22] https://youtu.be/GYv4Fs7nzIY

[23] Kara Tippetts, *The Hardest Peace: Expecting Grace in the Midst of Life's Hard*. (Colorado Springs, CO: David C. Cook, 2014).

[24] Quotes here are Heidi's reflection of the book and not actual citations.

[25] Tippetts, p. 147

[26] Ibid., 117.

[27] Ibid., 114.

[28] Ibid., 90.

[29] Ibid., 65.

[30] Ibid., 118.

[31] Quoted in Tippetts, "The Hardest Peace," 137.

[32] Ben Klrk, Jonathan Hively, Josh Smith, Justin Ebach, Rob Tahan, Ryan Nalepa, "Here for a Reason," © Wordspring Music, LLC (a div. of Word Music Group, Inc.); Ashes Remain Music (Admin. by Music Services, Inc.); Fair Trade Global Songs (Admin. by Music Services, Inc.)

[33] Kara Tippets went home to be with the Lord on March 22, 2015.

[34] https://youtu.be/NvZFjFNcINI; http://www.mundanefaithfulness.com/

[35] Pictures appear throughout this volume

Made in the USA
Lexington, KY
10 June 2018